A LOVE LIKE NO OTHER

MY TIME AS CAREGIVER:
SEVEN MONTHS OF GRIEVING
AND HOW IT CHANGED MY LIFE

*TO HANNAH
WITH LOVE!*

Kyle Helwege

BOOKS BY LYLE E. HERBAUGH

You're Not Smart Enough to do That
Stories from my life

Doubt and Redemption

Is That Love or What?
Gerda's Story

A Love Like No Other

A LOVE LIKE NO OTHER

MY TIME AS CAREGIVER: SEVEN MONTHS OF GRIEVING AND HOW IT CHANGED MY LIFE

BY

LYLE E. HERBAUGH

www.bookstandpublishing.com

Published by
Bookstand Publishing
Morgan Hill, CA 95037
4615_2

ISBN 978-1-63498-671-7

Printed in the United States of America

PREFACE

I Love You

I lie awake in the dark
I can hear you breathing
There beside me.
I reach out my hand
Gently touch your arm.
I whisper "I love you"

I come in from the garden
I smell the scent of
Sautéing garlic wafting
From the kitchen as you
Prepare dinner.

I kiss the back of your neck
I detect the unique smell
That I have grown to love.
A blending of shampoo,
Deodorant and your body.
I whisper "I love you".

A hundred times a day
I share my thoughts my
Desires and my dreams
With you. You understand,
You love me, you believe in me.

Memories flood my mind
They fill my heart.
Tears well up in my eyes
For memories are all that remain.
I will grieve your passing for a time.
But my whispered "I love you" is forever.

By Lyle Herbaugh

ACKNOWLEDGEMENTS

The nursing staff at the Cancer Care Center in Mount Vernon, for their care of Gerda during the year and a half of her journey. They are the most wonderful, caring, and compassionate professionals I have ever known. Her Oncologist, who is an outstanding doctor and a true gentleman. Gerda loved him and trusted him completely. During the last month of Gerda's life, the Hospice of the Northwest staff were indispensable. They made everything bearable by ensuring that she was comfortable and at peace. Everyone, from the intake nurse to the one who was with me at 4 a.m. that morning when Gerda passed, were caring, compassionate professionals. During bereavement counseling it was suggested that I write this book as part of my grief recovery.

PROLOGUE

If you or your loved one has been diagnosed with a terminal illness and you have decided to spend as much time as possible at home with your soulmate, whether as caregiver or patient, you are not alone. You are starting down a road that neither of you have traveled before, and one that will end in death and separation. It is not an easy road and there will be many potholes in the way, but it must be traveled. There are many alternative pathways, but they all converge at the end of the journey. There is no turning back, no matter how much you wish for a different ending, you must travel this one, the only one you were given. We chose to stay at home and be together until the end.

It happened to us, suddenly, without warning. My wife was diagnosed with Acute Myeloid Leukemia (AML), for which there is no cure. We were confronted with the same dilemma you now face. She was going to die. How and when, no one could tell us. What lie between now and the end were all questions to which there were no answers. What was going to be would be, and we had no choice but to deal with things as they appeared.

There were many decisions to make regarding her care. Hospital, skilled nursing, in home care with visiting nurses, plus many others. Choosing which option was influenced by the expenses we would incur. However; we had excellent health insurance and I was healthy and capable, so we chose to stay at home and be together as long as possible, and I would be her caregiver.

This book explains what we did, what we thought and how we reacted to each new circumstance that arose. It will not tell you what to do, or how to face each situation, because no two stories are exactly alike. It will, however; make it clear that others have traveled this road and perhaps their experiences will help you make your own decisions. No one can make them for you but knowing what others have done might make some of them easier for you in your time of sorrow and stress.

One essential part of this journey is love. Love for the patient and love for the caregiver. Whatever love you may feel at the beginning will change along the way. You will grieve as you travel and you will feel sorry for yourself, but that is normal. When you near the end you will find that you both have a love that is like no other you have ever experienced.

Sometimes the knowledge that one of you is going to die soon, rekindles the love that once brought you together many years ago, and it will be a love like no other.

This story takes you from diagnosis to death, and then through the first seven months of grief and recovery. Hang on tight because the road is bumpy and the direction is not always clear.

INTRODUCTION

It all started two years ago. My wife Gerda and I had celebrated our 55th wedding anniversary in April. We were retired, happy and looking forward to growing old together. Then the diagnosis of Acute Myeloid Leukemia (AML) rocked our lives. My wife had an incurable disease and was going to die. The question was, how long did she have, what would be the quality of that time and how would it end? If we did nothing she would be gone in about three weeks. If we treated it, maybe four to six months. She decided to fight and it lasted 19 months. Wow!

Looking back, it seems like a lifetime ago. Living it, things moved at an accelerated pace. It was always one flurry of activity followed by another. Appointments, medication, illness all running together into one long clutter of activity. Following her death life slowed down to where hours seemed like days and days seemed like weeks. I had time to waste and nothing to do. I had no purpose. There was no reason for me to even exist. I am getting ahead of myself, so let's go back to the beginning.

To understand the depth of my feelings and the strength of our union you need to know our story and how we got to this place in which we found ourselves.

To get to the beginning of our relationship you have to go back to 1945 when WWII ended in Europe. My wife was born and grew up in Germany. My cousin in the occupation forces and met my wife's sister. They married in 1949 and moved to Mount Vernon. I was 13 years old when I first met her. In 1956, I was in the Air Force and was home on leave. My wife's mother was visiting from Germany and I met her at a family picnic. She spoke very little English and I spoke no German, but we talked, waved our arms and made a lot of gestures, and I felt like we were communicating, at least a little.

From there I went to Okinawa, Japan where I stayed for two years. In 1959, I was assigned to Wiesbaden, Germany so while I was home on leave, I visited Irmgard and asked her for her mother's address and said that I would like to drop in and say hello. Irmgard, not only gave me the address, she showed me a picture of her sister. I was smitten and knew that I was looking at my future wife.

I visited with her mother and I met my wife. We started dating and five months later, in April of 1960, we married in Basel, Switzerland. This was the start of a 57-year romance. But this is not the story of our life together (I told that in "Is That Love or What: Gerda's Story") This is the story of what it is like to take care of someone whom you dearly love, who is terminally ill, watching them fade away and die. It is the story of the grief that follows and the effect it has on the health, both mental and physical, of the caregiver and griever.

CONTENTS

Preface: I Love You..v

Acknowledgments vii

Prologue..ix

Introduction xi

PART I – THE ILLNESS 1

Chapter One: The Diagnosis 3

Chapter Two: Treatment Begins 9

Chapter Three: Getting Organized 13

Chapter Four: Caregiving...17

Chapter Five: Normal Life, Almost...............................21

Chapter Six: My Health...27

Chapter Seven: Treatment Continues.............................31

Chapter Eight: Decisions..35

Chapter Nine: Treatment Ends 41

Chapter Ten: Hospice 45

PART II...49

Grief Recovery 51

Dear Gerda: Letters to My Wife....................................55

Ending 111

About the Author...113

PART I
THE ILLNESS

Lyle E. Herbaugh

1

THE DIAGNOSIS

September 23, 2015, a warm and pleasant fall day. Not too hot and not too cool. We had been called by our primary care physician and asked if we could come to his office, he needed to talk about some lab results he had received. Two days prior Gerda had blood drawn for her annual physical and we expected a high A1C. She had type two diabetes and had not been dieting the way recommended by the medical folks. We had no reason to suspect that something dark and ominous was going on in her body. She was not ill, or overly tired. She didn't have the stamina she used to have, but she was going to be 77 in December and nobody expected her to run a marathon.

When the phone rang, I could see that it was her doctor calling, so I asked her to take the call. I listened in on the extension phone.

"Gerda, this is Doctor Creelman. I have the results of your blood test and I need to talk to you about it. Can you come in the office today at 2 p.m.?"

She looked at me and I nodded my head yes.

"Yes, I think I can come. Why? Is there something wrong?" She wanted to know.

"Yes," he replied "but I don't want to talk about it over the phone. I will see you at 2."

She turned to me and said "my A1C must really be high for him to want to see me right away."

I agreed. "All we can do is speculate, so there is no reason to worry about it now. We will know soon enough."

As soon as we arrived Gerda was taken to an examination room where she met with Sondra, the ARNP who had been treating her diabetes. The doctor came to the waiting room and asked me to come with him. We went to the treatment room where Gerda was waiting. He never mentioned her A1C, but went right to the results of her annual CBC or blood evaluation.

"Your red cells are ok, but your white cells are way too high and your platelet count is very low. You have only 73 when normal is between 150 and 400. There is something going on in your body that we need to find immediately. Take this slip to the lab next door and they will expedite the results. I will call you when I get them."

"This must be serious if you need results so fast." I stated.

"Yes, it can be very serious. It could be cancer, but let's wait for the results of this test. I will call you as soon as I know something."

We left his office with a sinking feeling in the pit of our stomachs. The lab is right next to the doctor's office so we went there first. They drew blood and told us they would expedite the results.

Driving home Gerda was silent and I was scared half to death. *If the doctor is so worried and wants test results right now, it must be bad. The only thing I can think of that is related to blood is leukemia. Dear God, it can't be that.* I thought. I didn't say anything because I knew Gerda must be worried enough without bringing up the idea of leukemia.

We were home for a little over two hours when the phone rang. It was Doctor Creelman. I answered.

"The pathologist from the lab in Seattle called me and he is very concerned. It looks like Gerda has leukemia and it is fast moving. I called the Cancer Care Center in the Skagit Valley hospital and talked to the doctor on duty. You have an appointment at 10 a.m. tomorrow."

"What kind of leukemia are you talking about?" I asked.

"Let's let the oncologist make that determination, but it is not good news when the pathologist calls with the test results." He assured me.

"Thanks doctor, I'll stay in touch."

I hung up the phone and told Gerda what the doctor had said. She turned pale but didn't say anything. Neither of us slept well that night.

We met Doctor Kojouri the next morning at ten. We both immediately liked him. We talked about her past medical history and the symptoms that lead up to the blood tests. One of the things he wanted to know was did she ever have something called *Myelodysplastic Syndrome* (MDS). Neither of us had ever heard of MDS so he explained that it was a blood disorder that damaged the bone marrow and inhibited the production of new blood cells. It sometimes led to *Acute Myeloid Leukemia* (AML). After discussing the blood results, he told us that he needed to do a bone marrow biopsy, and that he had time to do it right then. Gerda had heard stories of how painful the test was and was a little hesitant to do it. Doc.

Kojouri explained that he could not get an exact diagnosis without it, and she said yes.

Doc. Kojouri was skilled and the biopsy was almost painless. He had distracted Gerda from the exam and she focused on his words and not on what he was doing. He told her that he would have the results in about three days.

I sent a text message to our three adult children, asking them to call me when they could. I said that it was important so please call as soon as possible. Each one called within an hour and we explained what was going on. Each one took the news in their own way. I told them that I would contact them as soon as we received the final diagnosis.

Three days later, we were in Doctor Kojouri's office waiting for the results. His face was very solemn when he came into the room and we both knew the news was not going to be good. He got right to the results. Yes, she had MDS and it had progressed into AML. He explained that there was treatment for both diseases, but that the survival rate was very poor when someone had both, especially in older people. (that is anyone over 60) He also explained that the treatment would not cure the AML but could extent her life for an unknown period.

I asked him what that meant in real time. He told us that if we did nothing she would die within a few weeks. If the treatment worked it could extend her life for about four months, but maybe a little longer.

The first treatment option was radical chemotherapy which would attack the cancer cells directly, but it would require a month in the hospital, and the probability that she would not survive the treatment was very high.

The second option was a series of injections of a drug called Vidaza, which entered the DNA of the cancer and switched off the gene that directed the cells to multiply. The drug was approved for treating MDS but was not yet approved for AML.

I called the kids and gave them the results of the biopsy and the proposed treatments.

I went online and researched everything I could find on the disease and the proposed treatments. The three kids did the same, and we all came to the same conclusion. Go with the Vidaza. She would receive injections every day for seven days, and then have 21 days to recover and then repeat the cycle. This could go on indefinitely.

Lyle E. Herbaugh

2

TREATMENT BEGINS

Gerda started the injections the following day. The list of side effects is long and scary. Doctor Kojouri told her that many patients tolerated it very well, so we were both optimistic and worried about what was coming next. She was nervous and I was concerned that she would suffer from the chemo.

It was the day of her first injection. We checked in at the front desk and were directed to the lab for a blood draw. Everything is in one area so no walking around looking for something. In about 30 minutes a nurse called Gerda's name and asked us to come with her. I was asked to come too, because everyone needs moral support the first day. We were taken to a long room with windows all around making it light and open. Along the side of the room were 16 reclining chairs for the patients and other chairs for the visitors.

The nurses were angels incarnate. They were gentle and caring and we both immediately felt like they truly cared about her as a person and not just as a patient. I cannot stress enough how important it is that you like and feel comfortable with the doctor and the nurses.

Gerda was very anxious about what was going to happen to her. April was the name of the first nurse who treated her. April made her feel comfortable and talked her through the injection procedure. *This is going to be tolerable,* we both thought.

We went home and waited for something to happen. We both expected some side effect to manifest itself at any moment. Nothing happened. The next three days we repeated the procedure at the cancer center. Each day she had a different nurse provide the treatment, and soon learned that all the nurses were caring compassionate people. We waited for some side effect but all that happened was itching and soreness around the injection sites. April recommended that we buy an over-the-counter cortisone cream and apply it liberally to the injection area. It worked very well and we were pleased with how things were progressing.

Five days into the first treatment series Gerda came down with double pneumonia and was hospitalized. The next day the hospital doctor told me that Gerda would not make it through the day and would go into respiratory collapse and die by evening. I called our son Gerald and his wife Betsy and asked her if she would call the other two. They all rushed to the hospital and waited. Over the next three days we waited and Gerda hung on. We had some decisions to make. She had not completed the form giving directions for life sustaining treatment. I was listed in her living will as the person to make those decisions. We gathered as a family and discussed the treatment options with the medical staff. We concluded that they should continue to treat her pneumonia but do not intubate her, and if her heart failed, let her go. That was the hardest decision I have ever made, but I knew she would want it that way.

She has no memory of those first five days in the hospital, and that is just as well. It was a struggle to keep her alive, but I believe God had a hand in her recovery. During her stay in the hospital she continued to receive the Vidaza injections.

A few days after the diagnosis our primary care doctor went on vacation to Texas. While he was there he called me every day to see how things were progressing with Gerda and if there was anything he could do to help. We were both impressed with the level of caring he showed for her.

I had called my niece and others I knew who believed in the power of prayer. They all prayed. I have no idea how many prayed for her recovery, but it was a host of folks.

After eleven days, she came home. She was on oxygen for two weeks, and had a visiting nurse and physical therapist come in several times a week, for a month. I cooked, cleaned house and did all the things around the house. Together we made shopping lists and I did the shopping. She rapidly regained her strength and interest in life. At the end of the month Gerda was doing many of the things she had always done. She took over the cooking and much of the housekeeping chores. The fantastic thing is that she had very few side effects from the injections. Life was almost normal, but not entirely. Her platelet count was low so she bruised easily. Her hemoglobin was low so she was anemic and needed transfusions.

When she was diagnosed with terminal cancer I was angry. First, I blamed God because I was always taught that God had a master plan and that we were along for the ride. This meant that God intentionally caused her to suffer and die. I didn't bargain with God, and I didn't get depressed, but I eventually accepted that He had nothing to do with her illness. The body just grew old and succumbed to a disease. As soon as I accepted the fact that she would die and there was nothing I could do about it, I turned to loving her and caring for her in the best way I possibly could. Caring for her became my purpose in life. Nothing else mattered.

3

GETTING ORGANIZED

The AML and the injections almost destroyed her immune system, so we had to be very careful not to expose her to any outside illnesses.

Dr. Kojouri gave us some dietary restrictions to help avoid contact with any contagions. Anything that was going to be cooked was ok, but anything that would be eaten raw had to be sterilized by washing them with water and rinsing in a mild Clorox solution. We thought that we would taste the Clorox, but when sufficiently rinsed, we couldn't taste it.

Gerda wore rubber gloves whenever she worked in the kitchen. I bought sanitary wipes to clean the counter tops and any surface that either of us might touch. Refrigerator, microwave, cutting boards, cabinet doors, anything we came in contact with. When preparing food, we used a lot of paper towels for drying and for keeping food items from touching the bare counter top. We didn't know what might have found its way onto the counter top since we had sterilized it.

We moved all potted plants into the garage just in case they might contain mold, mildew or other fungus. For the same reason, I could not bring any cut flowers into the house, no matter how much we wanted to.

At first the restrictions seemed difficult to deal with, but after a few days it became second nature to both of us.

There were many things that I had to take care of. The treatment was affecting Gerda's memory and she sometimes had to search for words. She couldn't keep track of her medical appointments, so I managed the calendar for her. The schedulers at the cancer care center did their best to make appointments at the same time each day, but that was not always possible. They had to schedule by type of cancer, how long the treatment would take and how many chairs were available. The center was functioning at full capacity, so it was not always possible to make a schedule that satisfied everyone.

Her medications increased. She was treating her Type II Diabetes when the cancer was discovered, so she had to continue with that treatment. For her cancer, in addition to the injections, she was given medication to counter nausea which made her constipated, so she required a stool softener to counter the constipation. Antifungal, antiviral, and antibiotic medications were all added to the regimen. Some of them had to be taken in the morning, some at noon and some at bedtime. Some were taken with food and some without. It became my task to sort and administer the medications at the right time of the day and with or without food.

I put everything in a spreadsheet showing what, how much, and when each medication should be taken. Then I went to the drug store and bought a pill box with four slots per day and seven days of the week. Each Saturday I checked my spread sheet and filled the pills in the proper box. With everything that was going on it was very difficult to remember if the medications were administered, so the pill box was perfect. When the lid was open the pills were gone, and if the lid was closed, I had forgotten. The next thing in pill management was to schedule refills in a timely manner so that she didn't suddenly run out of medication over the weekend.

The last big thing I needed to worry about was her vital signs. We were told to monitor her blood pressure, temperature and oxygen saturation at least once a day. I prepared another spreadsheet and tracked them. I also added the blood-sugar readings and the amount of insulin administered. I then printed out charts and graphs which I gave to the doctor at each visit. He kept them as part of the medical file. He liked them because it gave him a close evaluation of her general health. Caregiving was becoming a full-time job.

4

CAREGIVING

In November, Gerda completed her second round of Vidaza, and again had few side effects from the treatment.

We usually celebrate Thanksgiving at Gerald and Betsy's place, along with the other kids and their families. We asked the doctor and he said it would be fine to go, but if anyone had any symptoms of a cold or flu, to stay away from that person. He advised Gerda to wear a mask, but it is hard to eat Thanksgiving dinner with a mask on, so she ignored the advice most of the day.

Gerda's diagnosis overshadowed the day, but we had a wonderful Thanksgiving despite it. The whole family gave thanks for the things in our lives that were going well. We were all thankful that Gerda's treatment appeared to be working. We couldn't hope for healing so we hung on to what we had.

Over the next few weeks Gerda received platelet transfusions, and blood transfusions and continued her injections of Vidaza. The injections were given for seven days in a row, but the cancer center was closed on the weekends, making it necessary to go to the hospital and receive them as an outpatient. This was very stressful for Gerda. She knew and trusted the nurses in the cancer center but she knew nothing about the nurses in the outpatient clinic. What experience did they have in administering chemotherapy? How would they treat her and would they be as gentle and as caring as the cancer center nurses? It turned out that they were also skilled and caring folks and everything went without a hitch.

December arrived and she again took the Vidaza injections. This time Dr. Kojouri decided to skip the weekend shots and continue the following Monday and Tuesday. This made things much easier because we had the weekend to ourselves. Gerda needed several blood transfusions, but otherwise she was almost normal. She did most of the things she had always done, and I filled in helping with the things she could not do.

Christmas was fast approaching, and we brought the tree in from the garage and put it in the living room. We unpacked all the Advent and Christmas items and Gerda decorated the tree. I took her picture and then went into the bathroom and cried. All I could think of was that *this was going to be our last Christmas together.*

Together, Gerda and I made cookies and prepared for the holidays. The family was here for Christmas Eve, and Melinda and Sophia stayed for Christmas Day. Gerda was able to prepare the typical Christmas food. We had a special time sharing our love for each other. Somehow Gerda's illness has rekindled our deep and abiding love for each other, and for the children. It is the silver lining of a very dark cloud.

January 16, 2016. Some days are great, but some days suck. Today Gerda is having a bad day. She had a platelet transfusion yesterday, and to keep from breaking out in hives, she took Benadryl. This makes her so sleepy that she feels like she is in slow motion. This morning she wanted to make some vegetable soup and was cutting the veggies. Suddenly she became nauseous and weak. Broke out in a cold sweat and just felt terrible. In a few minutes it passed and she lay down and was soon sleeping.

When she has a bad day, I have a bad day, but I can't show it. It turns my stomach and I want to cry, but I smile, take her temperature and blood pressure, and give her encouragement. I can't talk to the kids about it because they are just as affected by everything as I am, so I just smile when I don't feel like smiling, I comfort when I need comforting myself. I pray when I think that God has forgotten about us and I don't hear an answer. Maybe He does answer, maybe He is healing her and I just can't tell yet. Maybe we will have many more years together. That is what I pray for, and that is what I live for right now, but when Gerda has a bad day, doubt rushes in and I don't know what to do about it.

Lyle E. Herbaugh

5

NORMAL LIFE, ALMOST

February 15, 2016. The platelet count was the first to return to normal, followed a month later by her red count and hemoglobin levels. She was no longer anemic. This ended the need for transfusions and restored a great deal of her energy. She was now able to function much the way she had before the illness. Our life was almost normal again except for her immune system. It remained very low necessitating caution in her interface with other people and causing us to avoid crowds.

We continued to wash and sanitize what she eats, and the kitchen. We still used soap and hand sanitizer by the bottle. It may have been overkill, but it was working. At first it seemed like a lot of work and too much bother, but it soon became the normal way to function and we did it without thinking.

During the time she was receiving blood transfusions iron began to build up in her liver. This is a normal occurrence and was expected to happen. Her ferritin count was elevated and we were told that when it reached 1000 she would be put on a medication to remove the iron and that her body had no means to do so on its own. The medication had a list of side effects that would scare you half to death, including loss of vision. I was very worried about her taking it. Her ferritin count rose to 927 and the doctor said that if it continued to rise she must start the medication. Her need for transfusions stopped and her ferritin count dropped on its own to 748. We were all thrilled. It continued to drop and on May 2, 2016, it was 686. The doctor didn't know how her body was processing the iron but it was and that is what counts. If she doesn't need further transfusions she should be good. We both believe it was an answer to prayer.

As we go forward we don't know how long the Vidaza will hold the leukemia in remission, but we hope and pray for complete remission. We live one day at a time. Gerda has handled her illness very well. She knows that with or without illness we are within a few years of dying, so the fact of dying is not a problem, it is how will she die. Together we hold hands and face the unknown.

June 3, 2016. Saw Dr. Kojouri today and he explained that he was very happy with Gerda's recovery and that the prognosis had improved. She is in the middle of her ninth series of Vidaza injections and is scheduled for her 10th series to start on June 23rd. Most of her blood readings have returned to normal, and her immune system has recovered a little bit. Dr. Kojouri informed us that following her 12th series he would do another bone marrow biopsy, and see exactly what condition the cancer is in. We pray that it is in total remission, but we will continue to take life one day at a time.

During the past nine months, we have both thought a lot about death and dying. When it is staring you right in the face it is hard to ignore. We both feel that our spiritual life is in order and that if heaven exists we will be welcomed home. We both know that under all circumstances we are only a few years away from the inevitable, so that is not the issue. Who will be left behind is a worry. A few months ago, it appeared that I would be the one, and that I would have to learn to live without her. Now we don't know, but whoever it is, it will be tough to make the adjustment. We have spent over fifty-six years together and for the last twenty-two years we have been together twenty-four hours a day, seven days a week. But each of us must die alone. It is frightening to think that one of the most important events in your life must be faced alone, without the partner you love and trust above all else. We are connected in ways that young people find difficult to understand. Whatever happens it will be challenging to cope with, but what choice do we have? Hang on, pray, and enjoy the time we have together to the utmost.

June 23, 2016. Gerda started her 10th series of injections. She had blood work done and we got the results the next day from Dr. Kojouri. Many of the readings were normal and he explained that he was not worried about the other ones. He explained each one again, and why he was not concerned. He then scheduled her for the 11th series.

Each time she starts a seven-day series of injections she has some side effects. For the first two days, her teeth hurt, the injection sites itch and are painful. We found a cortisone cream that really helps so she applies that liberally to the sites every evening. She takes an anti-nausea medication (Zofran) before each injection, and it causes her to be constipated, really constipated. After some experimentation, she found that a morning dose of Mira-Lax helps everything move. It is still, never the less, painful. For the next five days, she is able to function pretty well, but the whole process beats her down, both physically and mentally. The week following the chemo, she recovers and then for the next two weeks we live life as normally as we can. We continue to pray for full remission at the end of the year. Maybe, just maybe the good Lord will grant us that. With the blood tests almost normal we even allowed ourselves to hope for full remission and for several more years together. Hope is always there even when told there is none.

July 1, 2016. The 10th series has been the most difficult for Gerda. Today she received the last shot in the series. She was emotionally very fragile and could cry about anything. She complained that she was cold, and I offered to get her a warm blanket. She said no thanks, and started to cry. At times like this we are both completely helpless. She doesn't know why she is crying and I don't know what to do to comfort her. In a few moments it passed and she was smiling again. Later in the evening we were eating homemade tacos when she suddenly started to cry and apologized that she could not help me clean the kitchen and wash the dishes. She just didn't have the strength to do it. I held her for a moment and assured her that it was fine.

Gerda is struggling to keep her blood glucose levels in check. It is cherry season and Washington cherries are the best in the world. She loves cherries. She loves all fruit, but cherries are her favorite. This is when reality catches up with both of us. We both know that this could be the last cherry season we will see together, and so what if her blood sugar is a little high for a few days. Gerda decided that she was going to enjoy her cherries and the rest be damned. I find no argument that would support doing otherwise, so I buy cherries and we sit together and eat them.

July 14, 2016: I will turn 80 on July 21, 2016 and Gerda is planning a family party on the following Saturday. I just want a family picnic with hamburgers and hotdogs, with some good potato salad. That is what she is going to do, but she wants this to be the best birthday I have ever had and she wants to give it to me as a present. She knows that I will never be 80 again, and that this might be our last birthday together. I didn't mean to put her under so much stress, but I know she wants to do it, and it will be a fun day. It will be great to have the entire family together again.

Lyle E. Herbaugh

6

MY HEALTH

I have been having some problems with my heart. The rhythm is a little off, and when I monitor my pulse it feels like it skips a beat. The doctor explained that it is not life threatening, and I should not worry about it. I worry about it anyway. The problem is that Gerda worries more than I do and that puts her under additional stress. I have also been having a lot of pain in my left knee, which causes her to worry more about me. She doesn't need more stress, and it does not help her healing process. That causes me to worry about her which doesn't help my healing processes, thus the endless cycle goes on, around and around.

August 1, 2016: The pain in my knee stopped on its own and feels fine now. We were both relieved.

My birthday came and went and we both had a wonderful time. The family gathered and we spent the day celebrating. It was a fantastic love filled day. It was special for both of us. There were 15 of us and we ate a lot of hamburgers and wieners. Gerda made a great potato salad and tried a new recipe for pasta salad. Both were delicious and I ate more than I should have. Ron, Melinda and Gerald all helped with the cooking, set-up and serving. I was full to the point of being uncomfortable by the end of the day. It could not have been a better day. It was perfect.

My heart rhythm still bothers me and that upsets Gerda. I wore a Holter monitor for 48 hours and the results were declared to be normal. I have an appointment with a cardiologist on Aug 15th and we will discuss the meaning of "normal".

We saw Dr. Kojouri on August 2nd and he explained how he expects the future to play out for Gerda. She will complete the 12th series of chemo the end of August and is scheduled to have a bone morrow biopsy on September 13th. The results of the biopsy will not change the treatment with Vidaza, and she will continue each month just as she has been. It will give us a better prognosis and understanding of how the cancer is reacting and help us to project how long her life can be extended.

We both have mixed feeling about knowing how long. The way it is now we just live from day-to-day and blindly accept that it could go on forever. We know it will not and that it will end one day, but do we really want to know when? We must decide by the middle of September so we can advise the doctor about how much to tell us. I hate to make this kind of decision, because I am having difficulty accepting that my life's partner will soon leave me and I will be alone with no one to share the joy of the flowers and sunsets and all the little things we have shared for over 50 years. It is terrifying. Do I really want to know how much time we have?

This summer the flowers have been very beautiful. Everything has bloomed in profusion providing the yard and garden with a flood of color and beauty. I am enjoying it, but I can't escape the feeling that this is God's way of telling us that it will be Gerda's last summer and he is making it extra nice for her. We should share the pleasure it brings.

Aug 15, 2016: I saw the cardiologist today and was pleased with the visit. He spent a lot of time with me and listened very carefully. He assured me that there was a cause for my irregular heart beat and he would do his best to find it. He also assured me that it is not life threatening and that there is no reason for me to worry. The Holter monitor results show that it is too soon to give me a pace-maker, but that I will probably need one someday.

Gerda was very relieved that the cardiologist was working with me to find the cause and develop a treatment plan. It took a huge burden off her shoulders.

Lyle E. Herbaugh

7

TREATMENT CONTINUES

August 30, 2016: Gerda finished the 12th cycle of Vidaza injections. During the past several series of injections, by the end of the series she was very fragile emotionally and was often upset by little things and cried more than usual. This time she was not. In fact, she seemed to have more energy than ever before. We hoped it was a sign that the illness was losing its grip on her and she was getting better. On Friday, the 26th we saw Dr. Kojouri but he did not schedule the next Vidaza injections. We didn't know what that meant, but we would find out after the biopsy.

September 13, 2016: The bone marrow biopsy was done today and it was not as easy as the first one a year ago. Gerda had time to think about what was going to happen, and then when she was called back for the procedure there was a new nurse assisting the doctor. She was in training and everything had to be explained to her, step by step. All of this made Gerda very upset and she had to be given a tranquilizer to calm her.

She was tired for the rest of the day. We will be told the results of the biopsy on Tuesday, Sept 20th. They also scheduled the 13th round of Vidaza starting on Monday Sept 19th. It appears as if this will be how we spend the rest of her life. We continue to pray for healing, but that might not be the answer we receive. No is also an answer.

September 20, 2016: Yesterday Gerda started her 13th series of Vidaza and had some lab work done. Today we saw Doctor Kojouri and received the news. First the blood work was not good. Her immune system was so low it was non-existent. The desired number for her ANC count (absolute neutrophils count) is 1000. Gerda had a reading of 72. On top of the immune system, the marrow contained 11% cancer. The doctor expected a count of somewhere between 2.6 and 22, so 11 was right in the middle. It meant that the cancer was not multiplying and gave some hope that the treatments would continue to be effective.

To treat the low ANC, she will start taking a new medicine on October 4th. It is called Neuprogen and is designed to increase the neutrophil count and build up the immune system. We hope and pray that it works.

Each Vidaza series seems to get a little more difficult for Gerda. By day six, she is very fragile emotionally, and doesn't have the energy she had when she started the series. I suppose that is normal for anyone receiving chemotherapy, but it is very hard to watch. I know there is nothing I can do to help, so I try and not get in the way, but do what I can to take some of the chores away from her. We keep praying for complete healing but only time will tell.

I believe that Gerda is the most courageous person I have ever known. I read somewhere that traumatic events that occur during the first six years of a child's life will stay with them for their entire life. There is no cure and they must learn to deal with the trauma symptoms when and however they manifest themselves. This is definitely true in Gerda's life. She is afraid of everything. In her mind, anything could explode; you could fall from a bicycle; a stick would poke your eye out; at any time, something bad could happen that had the potential to harm you.

Courage is not absence of fear; it is how you deal with your fear. Gerda mastered her fear. She refused to let it rule her life and she did whatever she was required to do. Right up until now. She has faced death from cancer and looked it right in the eye and said no, I will continue to live, and she has. For the past year, despite her chemotherapy we have had an almost normal life. She insists that she can do it and she does it. My heart is filled with admiration and love for this woman who looks at her fears and perseveres. Thank you, Gerda, from the bottom of my heart.

8

DECISIONS

October 12, 2016: Gerda's ANC had jumped up to 418, so Doctor Kojouri decided not to begin the Neuprogen but to continue with the Vidaza. He scheduled the 14th series to begin on October 17th. He explained that the chemo was beginning to lose ground to the leukemia and it was only a matter of time until it would stop working at all. He recommended that she continue with the treatment but not to look for a cure. It will continue to work until it doesn't, then Gerda must decide how much she wants to fight the disease.

November 1, 2016: She started the month of November with a blood transfusion. The first one since February 15th. That was followed by a platelet transfusion on Friday, November 4th. The blood work does not look promising because all the important readings are down. Gerda's ANC is around 90 which is very low. She is scheduled to start the 15th series of Vidaza on the 14th of November. We will see how things go during that series.

November 20, 2016: She is in the middle of the 15th series of Vidaza and has not required another transfusion. Tomorrow she will have lab work done, and we hope no transfusions. She has not been feeling well for the past few days. Very tired and emotionally distraught. She gets upset very easily and cries at the slightest little thing. She doggedly holds on and does her housework. She washes and cooks and won't let me do any of these things. I watch her and it breaks my heart. Gerda is suffering and I cannot do a thing to help her. I am so grateful that she is not in pain. I don't think I could deal with that. It is difficult enough just to watch her fade away.

Doctor Kojouri prescribed an antidepressant, Zoloft, to help ease the emotional stress and her anxiety. After about a week we noticed a difference in her behavior. Much to my relief, she is more relaxed and she no longer gets upset at the little things that bothered her before.

December 15, 2015: Gerda was scheduled to start round 16 of her Vidaza injections. The blood tests indicated that the treatments are no longer working, so further injections were cancelled. In late November, she had needed a blood transfusion and a few days later a platelet transfusion. All indications are that the leukemia is winning the war, and a different approach may be required. There is another chemotherapy drug, Dacogen, that is used to treat MDS but also has the potential to fight AML. We weighed the side effects against the possible extension of her life and decided to continue to fight and see if Dacogen works. It will take about three months to determine if it is helping. We realize that there is only about a 30 percent chance that it will help, but 30 percent is worth the gamble. Maybe we are grasping at straws, but we can't give up hope at this point.

December 18, 2016: We baked Christmas cookies today. For the past 20 years, we have made Christmas cookies together, and Gerda insisted that we do it this year. She mixes the recipe and I cut out the forms and make the spoon drops.

We made three types of cookies and some spicy baked walnuts. By late afternoon she was tired, but we both felt very happy with our days' work. We both smiled a lot.

The tree has been up for a couple of weeks, and we are looking forward to Christmas with the family. Gerald, Betsy, Melinda and Sophia will be here on Christmas Eve and Melinda and Sophia will stay the night and Christmas Day. Gerda is going to make good German potato salad with hot *Fleischwurst* for Christmas Eve and *Sauerbraten* on Christmas Day. Both are family favorites. It will be a good time despite what else is happening.

January 1, 2017: Christmas came and went but not the way we had planned. Sophia and Melinda both had the flu and were unable to come. With Gerda's immune system being compromised they didn't want to come and expose her to the flu. Gerald called and asked if Betsy's two grown kids could come for Christmas Eve. We love them both and were happy to have them spend the evening with us. It turned out to be a quiet Christmas. Gerda and I were alone Christmas Day. She read a book she had gotten from me and I did my annual puzzle.

This was the first time since Sophia was born that she and Melinda were not with us on Christmas. After seventeen years, we had become accustomed to sharing this time with the two of them, and without them it seemed like the house was empty and lonely.

Gerda started a new chemotherapy drug last week and it is infused every day for 10 days. Because the cancer care center is closed over the weekends, Gerda was admitted to the hospital and received her infusions while an inpatient. I spent New Year's Eve alone at home and she was alone in her hospital room. We were both asleep by eleven o'clock.

January 7, 2017: We took down the Christmas tree today and put the Christmas and Advent decorations away in the garage for another year. We are both aware that this was probably our last Christmas and New Year, so we were very disappointed that it went down the way it did.

Gerda's condition has slowly gone downhill and she requires frequent blood and platelet transfusions. The new chemo may help but it will take about three months before we can expect to see improvements in her blood condition. We continue to hope and pray for healing, but that has not happened yet.

She is starting to show the effects of so many blood draws and IV infusions. There are bruises in several places on both her arms and some on her legs and body. We don't know how long this will go on and when or how it will end. We only know that at some point it will end.

Through the months of her illness we talked a lot about our lives together. Despite the rough beginning we have had a wonderful life. There are so many happy memories that I am sometimes overwhelmed with emotion.

I remember the Christmases when the kids were little; the many vacations in Denmark with long walks on the beach and the evenings sitting by the fireplace eating popcorn. The many road trips crisscrossing the country, seeing deer and antelope by the hundreds; meeting so many nice folks everywhere we traveled. The man in Paris, Texas who served us cold watermelon and refused to let us pay because I was in the service; the sunsets; the beautiful flowers; the time spent with our grandchildren, and the times we just sat together doing nothing, saying nothing, each content to be with the other. So many memories.

Life has been good to us both and I am so pleased that we were able to spend our lives together. Gerda was an extraordinary partner to me and for all the years, wherever I stood, she stood beside me. Whatever I did, she supported me. She was always there for me. After 57 years, I say thank you from the bottom of my heart, and I love you very much!

Lyle E. Herbaugh

9

TREATMENT ENDS

The year 2017 started with the new chemo, and everything went downhill from there. The doctor started her on an iron chelation medication and the side-effects were severe. The combination of the two destroyed any quality of life Gerda had, and her physical and mental condition rapidly worsened.

She continued to receive both blood and platelet transfusions and began to feel a little better, then on January 27th, when we took her morning vital signs her temperature was 103. I called the doctor and he wanted to see her immediately. After a very short interview, he admitted her to the hospital. When she had completed the Directions for Health Care, she had checked the block "Use antibiotics if life can be prolonged." The hospitalist immediately started large doses of antibiotics. Blood cultures revealed that some bacteria normally found in the mouth had somehow entered her blood stream and sepsis developed. Nothing we did or did not do at home caused the illness. It was her weak immune system that was at fault. There was nothing we could have done to prevent it.

While in the hospital they continued to give both blood and platelet transfusions when needed. She responded quickly to the antibiotics and in just a couple of days she was feeling well again and wanted to go home. She was released on February 4, with instructions to check in with the cancer care center twice a week for blood draws and transfusions when necessary. Doctor Kojouri issued a standing order so that if her platelet count or her HGB reached a certain level, the nurses could order transfusions. We faithfully went to the cancer care center twice a week for the months of February and March. At first the transfusions were needed every week, but the rate increased and by the beginning of April they were given every three days. We knew that this was not sustainable, and that some major decisions would soon be required.

April 3, 2017 her vitals showed that she was running a fever, and the doctor admitted her to the hospital. Once again, bacteria had found its way into her blood and she had sepsis. Again, she was given large doses of antibiotics. She responded well and was sent home on April 7, 2017. We discussed her condition with Doctor Kojouri and it was clear that the treatment was no longer effective, and that we should consider transferring to hospice care. We could continue taking transfusions which would keep her alive, but there was no possibility that her condition would improve. We prayed for divine intervention and for God to heal her, but He chose not to, and her condition waned.

We were faced with the most difficult decision we had ever made. During our life together, we had made some major decisions but they paled in comparison to this one. If we chose hospice we were choosing death. We had known this since the diagnosis, but the day had arrived where we had to let go. Let go of hope. Let go of life. Let go of everything we loved and shared. Let go of each other.

We chose hospice, and on May 1, 2017 Gerda transferred to hospice care.

Lyle E. Herbaugh

10

HOSPICE

May 1, 2017. The harsh reality set in. We had passed the last decision point and the end of Gerda's life was looming on the horizon. It changed everything we thought about and everything we did. Hope of recovery was gone. All we could pray for was that hospice would take the necessary steps to make her remaining time pain free and comfortable. We knew very little about hospice other than they dealt with end of life issues so we didn't know what to expect. We were not disappointed. The total focus of hospice was to make Gerda comfortable and pain free and to make my job of caregiver as simple and uncomplicated as possible.

We received a phone call from someone at Hospice of the Northwest asking what would be a good time for the intake nurse to visit and take care of all the paperwork. We told her that we were home all the time and to just pick a date and time. That same afternoon the nurse came by and did the admission of Gerda. When she was finished we had a hospice team established including a medical nurse, a chaplain and a social worker. We had all the insurance issues taken care of and a schedule for the first week of treatment. We had determined the medical equipment we needed, with the option that if anything changed we could get one-day delivery of the required item. A very important issue was resolved. We were given the option of which doctor would be responsible for the hospice care; our primary care physician or a hospice doctor. Even though we had never met the person, Gerda chose to be treated by a hospice doctor.

The following morning a shipment of all the medical equipment we needed was delivered. That afternoon I was called and asked to go to the pharmacy and pick up the package of medications that the hospice doctor had ordered. Later that day a large package was delivered containing non-prescription items that we would need. Everything came together flawlessly. I was impressed.

The second day the medical nurse visited and spent about two hours with us. She examined Gerda and they talked at great length about her pain and about her mental condition. Did she understand what was happening and was she frightened or worried about anything. When they were finished it was very clear to both of us that nothing would be done to prolong her life. All medications and treatments were for the sole purpose of keeping her pain free and at peace.

Next the nurse and I went over all the medications and made detailed lists of what was to be used for which symptom, and how each medication was to be delivered. When I felt comfortable that I knew what was required of me she asked me to administer the first dosage of the appropriate medication. When I completed the task, she left us. She told us that she would come once each week, but if we had any questions or needed to see her we could call anytime 24/7 and someone would be there to help us. It was comforting for me to know that help was only a phone call away.

The next day the chaplain visited. What a wonderful caring person she was. Gerda immediately liked her and trusted her. After introducing myself and offering some refreshments, I left the two of them alone to talk. I don't know what they discussed but when I returned Gerda was completely at peace. When the chaplain was ready to leave the three of us held hands and prayed together. The visit by the chaplain was optional and Gerda had requested the visit.

This is when everything changed for me. Until now everything I had done was to assist Gerda in her recovery and treatment. I had not given up hope and my efforts were directed towards her living and her happiness. Now hope had been snatched away and my love for her overwhelmed me. Anything she wanted or even mentioned that she would like, as soon as possible I obtained it so she could enjoy it. It didn't matter if it was something to read, to eat or to drink, it didn't matter what it was, I got it and gave it to her.

As the days passed her care intensified. She needed more and more help in bathing, using the toilet, or getting dressed and undressed. She insisted that she get out of bed, brush her teeth, wash her face and then get dressed for the day. She wanted to be ready for anything or anyone that came up that day.

Our daughter took time off from work and helped me with the care so I could get away for a few hours and to go shopping for whatever we needed. This was a huge help for me and gave them an opportunity to have some very special time together. During the month the rest of the family and many friends visited. Each person had time alone with her and said whatever they felt they needed to say. From that standpoint it was a wonderful month.

As the month progressed we needed more help from hospice. Gerda could no longer take a shower so they sent in a person to bathe her. The nurse inserted a catheter and helped change the bed sheets. Twice I needed help during the night and didn't know what to do. The first time I called the nurse on-call and she came over immediately. Within 30 minutes of my calling she was there. The second time, Gerda was making noise with every breath and I couldn't wake her. I called the nurse and she came immediately. Gerda had just passed while I was holding her in my arms. She opened her eyes and I could see that it was over. I checked for a pulse and there was none. The doorbell rang. It was 4:15 a.m. when I answered the door and let the nurse in. She examined Gerda and confirmed that she was no longer alive.

I didn't cry, I just felt exhausted and empty.

PART II

Lyle E. Herbaugh

GRIEF RECOVERY

T he moment Gerda passed my life changed in ways I could not have imagined. I didn't know what to do with myself or with the adult children, so I sat around and felt sorry for myself. I talked to a bereavement counselor at hospice, and she recommended I either keep a journal or write letters to Gerda. I have never liked keeping a journal, so I elected to write letters. This part of the story is how I recovered from the loss of my beloved wife of 57 years.

I tell her things about my life: who visited, who called and just about everything that happened and how I reacted to people's kindness. If you don't know who it is that I am writing about, that is okay. There will be someone in your life who will be doing the same thing and saying the same words that I have recorded here.

Even though their advice and support are well meaning, much of it makes no sense and is sometimes painful. Friends and family members feel they must say something and it is difficult to know what to say, so they resort to the age-old comments we have been taught since childhood: "She's in a better place." "It was her time and God took her." "God had a plan for her." "Time heals everything." "You're young. You will find someone else." The worst one is: "I know how you feel." NO ONE KNOWS HOW YOU FEEL, even if they have suffered the same loss. No two people suffer in the same way.

The list goes on and on but none of it is helpful. The one thing that helps is the knowledge that someone cares enough to want to give you comfort in your time of pain and sadness. Hang on to that and don't turn away someone who loves you, and wants to help.

Some good advice I was given was to join a support group and spend some time with others who have suffered the same loss. I did and, in that group, it was okay to tell someone how you feel and know there would be no criticism. You could cry, wipe your nose and cry some more and no one objected or thought you were weak or less of a man. I enrolled in an eight-week course of Grief Recovery Methods offered by hospice. We had a text book and homework to do, and it was a godsend. More on this later.

How I experienced the grief is not how you will feel. At first it may seem that life has no purpose and that you exist only because you are still alive. Remember, there is more to life than just not dying.

Over the coming months you will struggle. The pain of your loss will be very real and it may seem that life is over and that you will never smile again. You will feel empty and think that your life has no purpose. As time passes you will find that life goes on. You will live your life one day at a time. So, find something, anything, you love and then do it. Get into life and live again and you will certainly discover your purpose.

You will have your own thoughts and emotions to work with, but you will do as I have done. You will laugh again. You will miss your life's partner very much and for a long time, but life does go on and with time all the steps you take in your grief recovery will pay off and your life will once again be in order.

Lyle E. Herbaugh

DEAR GERDA
LETTERS TO MY WIFE

Dear Gerda,

    June 12, 2017. It has been almost two weeks since you passed, and not much has changed. The bereavement counselor told me to write a letter to you and tell you how I am doing. I tried several times but I couldn't get past "Dear Gerda". I miss you so much. I feel empty and I have no purpose in living. I don't know how many times I have thought *"I can't wait to tell Gerda."* But I couldn't, because you are no longer here. Each time the knot in my stomach got bigger. In the evenings, I look at your chair, where you always sat to watch TV, and I cry. There are so many memories associated with that chair. We didn't need to talk, we were together and that was all that mattered. It was as if a beam of energy connected us: You knew what I was thinking and I felt your presence and your love. I cherish all the memories of our time together.

    The years of raising the family, working and playing, are all precious memories, but they pale in comparison to the memories of the past two years. From the moment when Doctor Kojouri told us that you had leukemia and there was no cure for it, I knew why I was alive. I was meant to be your caregiver and to take care of you. I accepted that task and I did my very best to make you comfortable, and to help you deal with the disease that was going to take you away from me. I tracked the hundreds of medical appointments. I counted and measured the many prescription drugs you had to take. You began to rely on me for all the tough decisions and to make the right choices for your health and welfare. I accepted the assignment with love and tenderness and did my very best for you.

When you entered hospice, I became truly dedicated to you and your welfare. Somehow this responsibility gave me hope and purpose and my love for you consumed me. I had no reason to be alive other than caring for you. All the old inhibitions fell away. It was not a problem to help change your underwear. It was not embarrassing to stand by your side when you went to the bathroom. It was not an objectionable task to help clean you when you fouled yourself. I was alive at that moment to do just that. My mission in life was clear, and I had a purpose.

On June 1, 2017, my purpose ended with your passing. I felt like an empty box that had been thrown into the recycle bin waiting for the truck to pick me up and crush me into some meaningless blob. I was in pain and ignored the pain others were feeling. Somehow, I thought your passing was only my problem and that I was the only person who was suffering. Our three children had just lost their mother and they were in extreme pain, but I could not see beyond my own self.

I love you and miss you very much.

With all my love,

Lyle

****

Dear Gerda,

The first week passed in a blur. My feelings were all over the place. I didn't cry very much, why I don't know, because I have never been so sad and alone. Our three kids are wonderful adults. They took care of me, and helped me make my adjustments despite their own sorrow.

They stayed with me for a week. Ron stayed and never left my side. Gerald and Melinda came almost every day and cooked for me, they shopped for me, they cared for me. I could not have survived without their constant love and understanding.

During that week, we talked to folks at Hawthorne about niches that would hold both of us when the time comes. We looked at the Veteran's niches and were told that we could not be placed together, but would each have our own niche. We would be separated forever. I knew how afraid you were when I left you in the hospital and how you hated to be alone. When I returned, your fears subsided and everything was all right again. I told the kids that there was no way I was going to put you in a niche by yourself.

We all visited the other cemetery and talked to someone at Kern's Funeral Home about the niches there. We all felt good about us being in the same cemetery as my parents, grandparents and sister. Melinda felt the "vibe" that she said was very positive and she liked it. So that is where we two will eventually reside. I am OK with that.

Hawthorne called and said the death certificates were ready and that we could pick up the urn containing your ashes. The four of us drove up to pick you up. They put the urn in a shopping bag and I carried you out of the office. The idea that I was carrying you around in a shopping bag hit me very hard and I started crying. Melinda took you and held you in her arms. In the car, she held you and wrapped the seatbelt around you. We got home and we placed the urn on the vanity beside the beautiful white tree Melinda gave you for Christmas. I put your picture in a frame and placed it beside you. I always thought it was weird for folks to keep the ashes of a loved one in their home, until we brought you home. It feels normal and comforting to touch you and tell you how much I love you and how much I miss you. I don't know how long I will keep you here with me so only time will tell.

I love you and miss you more every day.

With all my love,

Lyle

****

Dear Gerda,

Today, June 14, 2017 is Flag Day, so I put out the flag. You always liked it when we flew the flag on holidays and special days so I had to put it out. The act of hanging the flag brought back a flood of memories and I felt like the world was crushing me. I was having a panic attack and found it difficult to breathe. I did what the nurse showed you, breathe in through my nose and blow out through my mouth. It helped a little and I soon calmed down and could breathe normally.

I don't know why, but I miss you more today than I thought possible. I try to think of other things, but I can't get my mind off the fact that you are no longer with me and I am alone. Not only am I alone, I realize that it will not get any better, and that I will be alone for the rest of my years, however long that might be. I must think of other things and stop going where I am fearful and anxious. I pray every day for guidance and for peace. Maybe God doesn't listen to selfish prayers and doesn't answer them. I don't know. When we were healthy and happy, attending Avon Church, it seemed so easy to pray and to feel His presence. Now it seems like God decided He didn't want to hear from me any longer, and shut the door. I can knock all I want but no one answers. How many times did I pray for your complete healing? It was many, but did I ever get an answer? No! At least not one I knew was from God. I suppose He told me no at some point but I didn't want to hear it. In reality, no is also an answer, just not the one I wanted.

I have faith that you are in a better place and have complete peace and love, and that I will one day join you there. That alone gives me something to look forward to. Otherwise I see only a lonely future with little or no purpose. Thinking of you no longer suffering gives me comfort.

On a positive note, I started walking on the treadmill again. I only go slowly until I get in better shape. During the months of your illness I stopped exercising and developed some aches and pains that I didn't need. I have been walking every day for the past week and already my back pain is improving. It also helps me take my mind off thinking negative thoughts. I must keep going and improving because I can't stand the dark places I go.

I love you and miss you so very much.

With all my love,

Lyle

****

Dear Gerda,

It is Saturday, June 17, 2017 and I am having a reasonable day. Yesterday was not a good one, and I couldn't seem to stop feeling sorry for myself. All my thoughts were about my loneliness and my sadness of not having you here with me, to share things with. I went out and mowed the lawn and it didn't help. Every time I went past the window I could see the empty chair in the living room. You always waved to me and smiled, even when you were so very ill. Now nothing, and I realize that it will never be again. I hate that feeling. That is when I pray to God to give me peace and take the black thoughts, but nothing changes.

Helen invited me over for dinner so I spent the evening with her and Don. We watched the baseball game and talked about many things. Their company lifted a load off me and I felt better when I got home.

I slept well last night but got up at seven and was still tired. I ate something and lay back in my chair and took a nap. I felt better when I awoke, so I went outside and did the trimming around the lawn and pulled some weeds. I have a lot of things in the garden that need to be taken care of, so if that helps, I have a full week of therapy waiting for me in the yard.

Oh yes, Monday I will be attending a support group for widowed people. I hope I meet some nice folks and find some relief from my sorrow. I know that time is a great healer, and I know that you told me not to be sad, but I am sad and I feel that time isn't going to remove that sadness.

I love you and miss you so very much.

With all my love,

Lyle

****

Dear Gerda,

Today is Father's Day so Melinda and Gerald came up and spent the day with me. Sophia stayed home and spent time with her dad. Gerald brought some Rib Eye steaks and grilled them along with some peppers and other veggies. I ate more steak than I have ever eaten. I guess my appetite is returning. I have lost 12 pounds since you passed, and I want to keep losing about 15 more. The weight loss feels good and I don't get so out of breath like I did before.

Look forward to tomorrow and attending the support group luncheon. We will see how that goes.

I love you and miss you.

With all my love,

Lyle

****

Dear Gerda,

Today is June 20, 2017 and yesterday I attended the support group luncheon and it was a big disappointment. I met some real nice folks, but we didn't talk about anything, we just ate lunch and went home. The only thing I found is that they all laughed and had a good time, so time will eventually give me the peace I need to smile and feel happy again. I don't know how long that will take, but we will see.

They meet every Monday at noon, so if I go back to Kiwanis I will be unable to attend. Each Monday they meet in a different restaurant for lunch, and I find that a little expensive. At the first meeting I spent almost $20.00 just for lunch.

I also registered for a class on managing grief through hospice that will start on July 13. I hope it provides more help than the other one did. The main difference is that the one yesterday was only for widowed folks, and the hospice is for all types of loss and grief.

I keep plugging along doing everything in and around the house. Everything is much like it was when you were here. I can't go to bed with dirty dishes in the sink; I change the sheets every two weeks, and change the pillow case every week; I do laundry to ensure that I don't run out of underwear or socks. When I do laundry I always clean the lint filter, I arrange the whites and towels separate from the dark and colored wash. I remove the shirts from the dryer as soon as they are finished, that way I don't have to iron them. After watching you do things for over 50 years, I can do no other. I would feel that I was disappointing you if I became a slob.

I love you and miss you and I think I always will no matter what I do. That's alright because I don't want to stop loving you and I don't want to stop missing you. Loving you keeps me going right now.

I miss you and love you very much.

With all my love,

Lyle

****

Dear Gerda,

June 21, 2017: It is the first day of summer and the longest day of the year. There is blue sky and sunshine, but the temperature is a bit cool. From now on it is downhill towards Winter. I do not look forward to the gray and damp winter. My mood most of the time is rather gray and dreary and when the weather is the same it hurts me to think about you and our wonderful life we spent together. Since the sun is shining I should be happy and smiling, but I am not. I am alone, I haven't found a purpose for my life and I miss you terribly.

It has been exactly three weeks since you passed and I am as sad and down as I was the first week. I pray every day that the Lord will give me peace and take away the pain and darkness of my loss, but it is still there and it is very real.

Melinda calls almost every evening and we talk about things. It helps for an hour and then the sadness settles back into place. Ray and Gloria came down today and spent a couple of hours with me. I talked about caring for you and about your final months here with me, and it helped for a while. They no sooner left than I began to feel sad again. I know it will get better, but I wish it would hurry up.

I received another bill for $3,105 from the hospital that I am contesting. It is for things that are covered by insurance and should have been paid already. Every time I call the hospital about a bill, I must wait for a return call and it can sometimes take 72 hours for her to return my call. That means I must be available to take the call and can't leave the house even to go out and work in the yard. I don't like it but what options do I have.

Melinda and Gerald are making plans for your celebration of life we will be having on July 16th at Hillcrest Park. You had said to have it at Bayview State Park, but that would mean that everyone attending would have to pay the $10.00 parking fee. We were sure you would not want that. Through the years we have attended so many family reunions at the gazebo in Hillcrest, that it seemed like the appropriate place. It will be a pot-luck picnic open to family and friends. We will be saying I love you in a very special way.

On Monday, I have an appointment with Kern's Funeral Home to buy a double niche for the two of us. I don't have the heart to put you in the niche alone and I think I will keep you here with me until it is time for both of us to be placed in the niche together. That's my thinking right now. That could change, but I don't expect it to.

I love you and miss you.

With all my love,

Lyle

****

Dear Gerda,

Today is June 22, 2017 and it has been one of the worst days I have had so far. I thought I was getting better but I woke up today feeling sorry for myself and have not been able to shake the feeling. For three days, I have been waiting for Amy (the girl who handles the hospital bills) to return my call. Since it is important that I take her call I am stuck here in the house with nothing to do but think.

Oh yes! June 20th was Klaus's birthday. I sent him an email and the next day he called. He said he would have called sooner but your passing hit him and Gabi so hard that they could not talk about it. He had a very hard time talking without crying. He told me that he had told Hilda about it and she was also an emotional mess. Gerda, you have no idea how much you are loved and by how many folks.

I sent Rob and Joanie an email and told them the news. Rob immediately called me and we talked for a long time. He gave some words of encouragement which helped me a lot. I stopped feeling sorry for myself and looked closer at the wonderful times we shared with each other and with the family.

I continue to miss you and love you. I think I always will.

With all my love

Lyle

****

Dear Gerda.

Saturday, June 24, 2017: Summer is here and heat is forecast for the next few days. It should reach into the low 90s. I made a mistake not having air conditioning installed when we put in the new furnace. My bad. I will set up the fans and ride it out.

Melinda is coming up on Sunday for a few hours. She calls often and I really appreciate her concern and calls. She is struggling with her loss much like I am. Even though she didn't appear to on occasion, she worshiped the ground you walked on. I knew it all along and I think you realized it the last few years. I know the pleasure her accomplishments gave to you, and the praise you heaped on her for what she had done. That memory gives me pleasure.

Life without you by my side is lonely and meaningless. My day is filled with boring details of staying alive. The flowers are in bloom in the garden, the wild daisies are everywhere, but I don't care. I look at the ones that you loved so much, and I feel empty and alone because you are not here to share the pleasures with me. I suppose that is a selfish position to take, but I can't help it. We were one in the biblical sense. Your passing took half of me away and I don't know how to fill the void it created. Everyone tells me it will take at least a year to heal, but I don't feel that it will ever heal. Maybe, and I hope so because life without you is no fun at all.

I miss you and Love you more every day.

With all my love,

Lyle

****

Dear Gerda,

Sunday, 25 June, and hot. Melinda came up today and spent the day. I grilled some hamburgers and steamed some asparagus and broccoli. Everything was great. Right after lunch we got in the car and went to Michaels to buy some ribbon to use on the 16th. Then we went shopping in several of the stores in the outlet mall. I sat on a bench in the shade while Melinda was in the stores. I hate shopping, but I wanted to be with someone and did not want to be home alone.

We talked a lot about you and our lives together. Melinda has planned everything for your celebration of life. Red and white checkered table clothes on each table. In the center of every table will be a Mason Ball fruit jar with white Shasta daisies. They will be beautiful and I know you will love what she has done. It will be a wonderful day for the family. Everyone loves you so much and wants to say farewell in a way that is worthy of you.

I miss you

With all my love

Lyle

****

Dear Gerda,

Today is Monday, June 26th. I had an appointment with Kern's Funeral Home to talk about a niche for the two of us. I bought one on the eighth row. Everything below that was already taken, so I paid for what was available. Don't worry, I am not going to put you in a niche alone. You will stay right here with me until it is my time to go, and the kids can put us both in at the same time. That sounds so horrible but it is what awaits us.

Some days I believe my sadness is becoming less and I feel better, then the next morning I wake up and feel terrible again. It has not yet been a month and the sadness from you not being here to share things is still very real. The folks who are supposed to know these things say it will take a lot longer than a month, and I am sure they are right. I am not ready to start clearing out the house and giving away your things. Everything reminds me of you, but that is preferable to having your things gone with only my thoughts to remind me. It feels cruel to do that and I don't want to do it. So, I am not going to do it. Melinda said that when I am ready to do something she will come up and help me.

I miss you and I love you more every day.

With all my love

Lyle

****

Dear Gerda,

June 27, 2017: I went to foot care this morning. It is worth the money to have someone else trim my toenails because I have difficulty reaching my feet and having enough control to trim them.

Gerald came up today and spent the afternoon with me. The weather was nice so we sat out on the front porch most of the time. We went to the Red Apple and bought all the things that he needed to make his great lasagna recipe. It fills an 8X13 pan. He didn't want to take anything home with him so I kept enough for tomorrow and froze enough for three more meals. It feels good to have something in the freezer that I can just stick in the microwave and heat in a few minutes. Most of the time I don't feel like cooking something from scratch. Remembering how you used to prepare such wonderful tasty dishes and make it seem so easy, makes it difficult for me to try to cook. Don't worry about me not eating enough because I am not losing weight, so I must be doing something right.

Tomorrow I am going to go renew my driver's license. It should go ok. I drove past the Department of Licensing in Mount Vernon and the parking lot was full. Helen suggested I go to Anacortes and get it done there. I might do that.

Days all seem to run together with nothing changing. I know I must find something to do and to be with people, but I haven't felt like doing it. You always said that I should go back to Kiwanis and I believe you are right. I plan to start attending the meetings next Monday.

God, I miss you and I love you unconditionally.
With all my love
Lyle

****

Dear Gerda,

I went to Anacortes and renewed my driver's license. I walked in and there was no one waiting. I walked up to the counter and in about five minutes I had my new one and I left.

68

What a difference. The new one is for six years, so maybe I will not have to renew it again. Time will tell.

Today is Thursday, June 29, 2017, and I have an appointment with Dr. Lo, the cardiologist to get the results of the Holter monitor I wore for three days. That was over six weeks ago so I assume it was normal, with nothing to worry about.

The last two times Melinda was here, Sophia didn't come with her. She had something else to do. Yesterday evening she called me and we talked for 20 minutes or so. It was really nice and I enjoyed our talk. I hope we can stay in touch because she is such a wonderful young lady.

When I get home from the doctor's office I will let you know how things went.

I just returned from the doctor's office and my Holter monitor results are normal. I had only one short session where my heartbeat was irregular. It is the same rhythm I had before and is not life threatening. He told me to get back into life and not to worry. I will try and do that. I am to make an appointment in six months.

While I was there I bumped into April in the hall. We talked for a long time. She was so understanding because she took care of her brother and sister and watched them pass on. One of them was her twin and it was hard for her. I told her that I didn't have a purpose and was searching. She assured me that I did have a purpose and I should pray for it and then accept it no matter what it is. I will wait and see. It was nice to talk to her though.

I love you and miss you.

With all my love.

Lyle

****

Dear Gerda,

Today is Saturday, July 1, 2017. It has been one month since you passed on to be with the Lord. I pray every evening asking Him to take good care of you until I get there. I pray for peace also and I am still waiting. Everyone, including April tells me that it will take at least a year before I can expect to feel normal again.

I am not having a good day today. Don and Helen have been up in the woods since last Thursday and are leaving for Canada today. Today is Canada's Independence Day and Tuesday is ours, so they will be celebrating both days. I see very little of them. I guess they expect me to call them if I need something, but when you feel bad you don't want to dump on someone else so I don't do anything. Maybe I need to reach out to them a little more.

We were, in the biblical sense of the word "One". When you passed, one half of me was torn off and cast away, and nothing can fill the void it left. I talk to Tom and Georgia, and they can't fill it. Don and Helen can't fill it. The three kids try very hard, but they can't fill it either. I suppose only time will heal the wound. That is the hardest part of missing you that I must deal with. Every day I see or hear something and I think *"Oh wait until I tell Gerda."* When I mowed the lot, I found two tiny little rabbits hiding in the grass, just like the ones we found at Mike's place. I couldn't wait to tell you.

Gerda, I miss you so much, and love you more every day.

With all my love
Lyle

****

Dear Gerda,

It is Sunday today and I went to church. I went to the Bethany Covenant where so many of the old Avon folks started going. They are on Summer schedule so they have only one service on Sunday. The place was absolutely filled to capacity. I saw Jim from a distance, but not one of the other Avon crowd. I was a little disappointed but it was OK. The entire pastoral staff has changed except for Vickie Lund. The sermon was on the Fruit of The Spirit and was great. It made so much sense and the young pastor presented it so well. I was glad I went. It was a little strange because I sat in a room with 600 other people and I was still alone.

It was also communion, in which I participated. I cried the entire time, thinking about the times we stood beside each other and took communion. Every time something makes me think of our times together, and almost everything reminds me of you, I get lonely. I stopped feeling sad because this is the way it must be. I am alone and you will never be here with me again, and that just leaves a huge hole in my existence. If it is going to take a year, then I hope the year flies by, because it is hard to be without you. I don't want to make you unhappy, so don't listen to my complaining. I do love you and I know that I will always love you. Take care my dear. I know you didn't like it when I called you dear, but it now fits, because you are so dear to me.

> I love you and I miss you
> With all my love,
> Lyle

****

Dear Gerda,

Today started off very well. I slept well last night and was rested when I awoke at around seven. I immediately took the sheets off my bed and put them in the washer. They were done about the time I finished breakfast, so I put them in the dryer. I sat down in the family room and read for a while. When the dryer buzzed I took them out and spread them on the bed so they wouldn't get wrinkled.

In the next two hours, I vacuumed the entire house, dusted everything including the pictures; mopped the kitchen floor and both bathrooms. I put the blue stuff in both toilets and scrubbed them. I still need to make up the bed this afternoon, but that goes fast. I don't love doing these things, but I know you would have done them and I can't disappoint you, so I do them, mark the calendar, and two weeks later I do them again. It somehow helps me. Your love keeps me going and doing the things that need to be done.

Tomorrow is the 4th of July and Melinda is coming up to spend some time with me. We plan to go to Mount Vernon in the evening and watch the fireworks. I haven't done that for a long time and we think it might be fun.

I love you and always will. I miss you so much.

With all my love

Lyle

****

Dear Gerda,

Melinda came on the fourth and I made schnitzel for dinner. Turned out really good. Made some carrots and roasted peppers and broccoli in the oven. Nice meal. I did learn something from watching you cook all those years.

I started having pains in my upper abdomen on Monday and wasn't sure what was causing them. I tried Maalox and then a little later some Nitro. Both helped and the pain would go away for a couple of hours. I decided I needed to see the doctor and let him sort it out.

When I told Melinda about the pain we decided not to go to the fireworks. It was better because she had to get up at five to go to work, so staying here with me until 11 p.m. didn't make any sense. She went home around seven and I watched the celebration from Washington D.C. that we always watched. Without you here to share it with, it was no fun. I turned it off and watched something else before the fireworks started. I did, however, watch the show from Seattle. They put on a great display from Gasworks Park. Someone in the neighborhood shot off a ton of fireworks. They were pretty big ones so someone spent a lot of money just to make noise.

On days like the Fourth, when we have so many memories, I feel my worst. It is terrible not having you with me to share everything with. I know this too will pass, but I miss you so very much, and love you more every day.

With all my love,

Lyle

****

Dear Gerda,

Wednesday, July 5, 2017: Went to see Dr. Creelman today. He could not be certain which is causing my problem, stomach or heart. One year ago, I did the stress test and passed with flying colors. No indication of any blockage. Also, about two years ago I had the complete colonoscopy, and was told there was no problems. There were some small little pockets but nothing to worry about. He was stumped.

He gave me a series of tests to make using Maalox and Nitro, to see if I could isolate the problem. We will see. The pain is very mild and only bothers me when I walk. I can sit, lie and nothing. Get up and walk and I feel the discomfort. Oh well.

I need to get out in life again. I don't feel like it, but it is what everyone tells me. Maybe I will go to the Senior Center for lunch tomorrow. Thursday is when Ron goes to visit with his sister. That might be a good time to go. I will see how I feel when the time comes.

I love you Gerda, and I miss you every minute of every day.

With all my love,
Lyle

****

Dear Gerda,

Thursday July 6, 2017: I went to the Senior Center for lunch today. Ron was there and so was our neighbor Earl. We sat at the same table with Ron's sister, and had a very nice visit. Earl goes there every day. He eats lunch, but he said that the reason he goes is for the fellowship. I certainly understand that.

July 7, I went to Don and Alice's house for a reunion committee meeting, planning the next school reunion. It was nice to see the guys again. One of the women, Claudette whose husband Jack died about a year ago, was there. We talked briefly about our loss and she told me there was only one thing I could do and that is to take life one day at a time. I don't know what that really means, but I have no choice but to take it one day at a time.

Sunday, July 9: Melinda and Sophia came up and spent the day. They stayed overnight and I really enjoyed their visit. We went over the planning for your Celebration of Life and it is going to be a wonderful outpouring of love for you. You touched so many people's lives. I am amazed by how many folks have told me how you influenced them. It is so nice to hear.

Monday, July 10. Saw Doctor Creelman about my abdominal pain. It has gone and only happens occasionally. It comes and goes so fast I can't get a handle on it. I have decided that I have gas pains.

I got a call from David at Hawthorne Funeral Home inviting me to attend a men's group that meets the second Wednesday of each month. It is only for men who have lost their wives. I think I will attend.

I will let you know how it is. I love you and continue to miss you.

With all my love

Lyle

****

Dear Gerda,

Thursday, July 13, 2017: The men's group was very interesting and helpful. I met several very nice men who had the same feelings I have. The finality of your passing, and the loneliness that follows, seems to be a common feeling, especially with men. I will continue to attend and see how everything develops.

This afternoon I attended the first session of Grief Therapy, and really liked it. It is a study with a text book and homework that we must complete each week. It approaches grief the way I like to approach things. It will be once a week for eight weeks. I know it is going to be very helpful.

Friday, July 14: Ron and family are coming up today. They will be here until Monday, and are then going to Victoria, BC for a few days of vacation. Sunday is your picnic Celebration of Life. There are a lot of people who are going to be there. It will be a wonderful day. I am so glad it is happening. It would not have been right to just let things end with nothing. You have no idea how many people loved you.

I am one of them who loves you dearly, and who misses you every day.

With all my love
Lyle

****

Dear Gerda,

Sunday, we gathered at the Hillcrest Park gazebo for the picnic to celebrate your life. Melinda catered the event and it was beautiful. White tablecloths with a red and white checkered pattern as a center place. In the center of each was a vase full of Shasta daisies. Everything was perfect. With family and friends there were 80 guests, not counting we four. Nurse Anne wrote a nice presentation, but she could not be there because they had vacation reservations in Eastern Washington. April read the paper on her behalf.

From my Club 54 friends there were six members, all with wives. Tom and Georgia couldn't make it. Six nurses from the cancer care center attended. Pat read a beautiful poem she had written. Dave and Nancy with Steve and Jo came. They didn't say anything but their sadness of your passing was evident.

Overall it was a fantastic love-filled day. Everyone who spoke, and there were many, praised your warmth and love, your wisdom and intelligence.

When it ended I was exhausted and couldn't help tear down and pack everything we had brought. It got done anyway. David and Carla came by the house before everyone had to leave and we had a wonderful visit. When they all left the sense of finality set in. I had a feeling of utter emptiness and loss. It is over. Our life together has ended, and I know that on this earth I'll never talk to you again. I'll never share a flower or a poem or a tidbit of news again. It is a terrible feeling and I hope and pray it passes very soon. I don't want to worry you with my feelings, but half of me is missing and I miss you, oh god do I miss you.

I love you more today than ever before, and I miss you more than I have since you passed.

With all my love

Lyle

****

Dear Gerda,

It is now Wednesday, July 19, 2017 and I am no better today than I was on Sunday evening. I am lost without you and it seems so final, like I will be lost forever. Intellectually I know that is not true, and that I will recover, but right now I am just a mess.

I went to the Senior Center for lunch today and they had a little country group singing songs from the distant past. I didn't like the music because I didn't feel like music, and I didn't care for country music before and I don't care for it now. I could hardly wait to get out of there. The food was alright and I had a good meal, but the atmosphere was not for me.

Earl was there and we sat together again. We didn't talk because the music was too loud. Every time I see him he seems to be in worse shape. He is really showing his age.

I spent yesterday evening with Don and Helen and it helped to lift me out of the funk for a few hours. We talked and watched the baseball game and it helped me. I had to call them and see if I could come over because the four walls were closing in on me.

Oh, I hope and pray that God gives me peace very soon. Missing you is driving me nuts.

With all my love, my dear

Lyle

****

Dear Gerda,

Yesterday was my 81st birthday. My first one without you. Gerald and Betsy came up and Hannah and Mikah came down from Bellingham. Gerald made chicken schnitzel with pepper sauce. He made a lot so we had leftovers.

Ron and Marisa returned from Canada late in the evening. Today before they left we ate left over schnitzel and whatever else we could find in the frig. It was nice, and the company lifted me out of the doldrums a little.

The thing that helped me the most was the grief recovery program on Thursday. I felt terrible when I went over to the hospice building, but after doing the exercises and talking to folks I felt better. I am glad that I signed up for the class because I am learning things I needed to know to recover from my loss.

I am still looking for a purpose and I don't see anything on the horizon. One day I feel like I am going to be OK, and then I crash again. I don't know of anything specific that causes the crash, I just suddenly feel bad, lost and alone. Maybe it is because I am alone that I feel it so strongly. I will keep looking and taking the good days as they come and dealing with the bad ones when they happen. Life without you is not fun, it is not even nice in any way. It is just a long lonely existence. I can't describe how lonesome I am and how much I miss you, so I won't try, but trust me, I miss you every second of every day. I think it will always be that way.

Every night I ask the Lord to take good care of you and to treat you with love until I can get there. I love you and miss you.

With all my love,
Lyle

****

Dear Gerda,

When we were setting up the gazebo for your celebration I hurt my back while moving picnic tables around the park. Over the next week it got a little better, but on Sunday I woke up in pain which lasted most of the day despite taking Tylenol several times during the day. Monday morning, I was still hurting so I went to see the doctor. He poked around and said that I had cracked a rib which would take 10 days to two weeks to heal. He told me "Just be careful and don't do anything that will stress the rib." Today it is much better.

Today is Wednesday, July 26, 2017 and I am going to attend the men's group luncheon at Hawthorne. I like Dave, the group leader and several of the men were nice to talk to. Speaking of lunch, yesterday I went to the Senior Center for lunch and didn't care for it at all. There are so many poor homeless folks there who talk all the time. It is almost impossible to have a conversation with someone without them interrupting and inserting their comments. They are usually trying to be funny, but mostly they are just dumb. Anyway, Martha was there and we sat together and talked as much as we could. The food was also very bad: over-cooked chicken, soggy over-cooked vegetables and a salad. I can do better than that myself, and don't have to put up with folks I don't want to be around.

You will be glad to hear that I am working on another book. I am writing a detailed account of the 19 months of your illness and my role as caregiver. And then in part II I will cover the first six months of grieving. Wendy, from Hospice suggested I write it, and when I asked April what she thought, she was enthusiastic about it. She said that there was nothing like that available and that it could be a big help to someone faced with the same situation. It is also therapeutic for me.

I hope and pray that you know how much you mean to me and how much I love you. I will always love you and miss you.

With all my love
Lyle

****

Dear Gerda,

Today is Friday, July 28, 2017. Wednesday, I attended the luncheon sponsored by Hawthorne, and it was a nice meeting. There were about 30 folks there, both men and women. Dave, the moderator talked about a book on grief which he praised as the best one he had ever read. The next day I ordered it from Amazon.

My ribs continue to be painful much of the time, especially at night when I lie on my right side. It is also difficult to lie on my back, but with lots of Tylenol I am doing better.

The Thursday afternoon Grief Recovery meetings are very good. I always feel much better when I leave them. I can't tell you what it is that helps me, but I don't feel so alone and anxious like I do much of the time. My feelings are very difficult to explain, even to myself. I get up some mornings and feel almost normal, or at least the way I used to feel, and then without warning, I suddenly become anxious and want to run. I don't, and in a few minutes the anxiety passes and I just feel alone. The thing I feel most is the sense that I am alone and will always be alone. Some folks like being alone, but I don't. I want to share everything with you, but I can't. I tell you anyway, but it is not the same. I long for your comments and feedback on whatever it is that I just told you.

I am forced to make all the decisions without your input. I don't know when I made a decision without discussing it with you beforehand. I don't have the security that whatever I decide to do is the correct thing to do. I always relied on your input and when you supported my position, I knew it was right. I don't like being alone.

I will miss you as long as I am alive, and I will never stop loving you.

With all my love,

Lyle

****

Dear Gerda,

It's the first of August and the past few days have passed in a fog. It has been hot with the temperatures in the high 80s. I get out early and water the flowers and then take a short walk. I go up to the top of the hill and then all the way down. If it isn't too hot I will walk up Hickok road and back. It usually makes me feel better but not always.

I made an appointment for my bone density scan. I go tomorrow at 9:30 a.m. I won't know anything until the doctor has read the scan and sent it to Doctor Creelman. I hope and pray that I don't have osteoporosis, but it could be. I can't say that I am worried about it, but I am a little concerned.

Amy called me today and asked if she could come over and spend a few minutes with me. She was running errands in Mount Vernon, and wanted to see how I was doing. We had a nice visit. She stayed for over an hour and we talked about a lot of things. We are both now alone and when we compared notes, she likes being alone and I hate it. She is coming out of something she didn't like and I am coming out of something I never wanted to end. The talk was helpful for me and it took away my sense of loss and loneliness for a while, so I felt much better because of her visit.

I don't know how to explain the feelings I have about being alone with no end in sight. It weighs on me and saps my energy to where I don't want to do anything. There is so much to do outside but I can't bring myself to go out and do it. Grieving takes a lot of energy. I never knew that, but at the grief recovery meetings almost everyone feels the same lack of energy.

I bring dahlias in every few days and put a vase of beautiful flowers next to your urn. I don't know how long I will do that, but maybe forever.

I miss you, I love you, and I will never stop doing so.

With all my love

Lyle

****

Dear Gerda,

Today is the 3rd of August and I drove my brother Don to a doctor's appointment. Helen was working and couldn't take him. He had an appointment with Dr. Crowell in Sedro-Woolley. They were going to dilate his eye and he didn't want to drive home. The weather was warm and the air conditioning in the office was uncomfortably cold. I had to go outside to warm up.

I had the Grief Recovery meeting today and we did something interesting. We started a graph of our entire lives starting with our first conscious memories and ending today. As our homework, we are to date every negative thing that has happened to us. Next, we determine how strong the loss was and explain how we felt about it. It will be an interesting but very difficult job to dig up old losses and evaluate them. I do like the classes and the people I have met there. It also helps me adjust to you no longer being with me. How? I don't know, but it seems to take the edge off. I am grateful for that.

It makes me realize that I will always miss you, but someday I will be able to do it without pain and heartache. I look forward to that day.

I love you and continue every evening to ask God to be kind and loving to you and to take care of you until I can join you.

With all my love.

Lyle

****

Dear Gerda,

Today is Sunday, August 6, 2017. Yesterday Don and I went to the Sager family reunion. It is always held on the first Saturday of August at Ken and Louise's place on the Nooksack River. It was a beautiful day and we both enjoyed it a great deal. It is sad that Bob is demented and requires constant care. To make the problem worse, Jan fell and broke her left arm at the shoulder. She is not in a cast, but the sling is firmly positioned against her side and she can't move the arm. She can't sleep in bed because it put pressure on the break.

I forgot to tell you but our neighbor Pat fell in her garden and broke her right arm at the shoulder, and she has the same restrictions that Jan has. The big problem for Pat is that she broke her right arm and she can't pull the lever on her recliner because she is right handed. Julie is taking care of her, but when school starts it will require some outside help.

Today is Amy's birthday. You had the date marked on the calendar so I remembered and sent her a nice card. I must transfer all the birthdays onto the new calendar at the end of the year otherwise I will lose track of everyone.

I made my loss graph for the grief recovery class and it turned out to be more difficult than I anticipated. It was quite easy to remember the events and approximately when they happened, but when I started writing about each of the events I got all emotional and had to quit. I will work on it again on Tuesday. I hope it is easier than today.

Somehow things seem to be getting better. My anxiety attacks are becoming farther apart, and I am grateful for that, but I miss you every day. I love you every day.

With all my love,

Lyle

****

Dear Gerda,

Yesterday was Monday and I saw Dr. Creelman and got the results of my bone scan. Good news, I don't have osteoporosis. My spine is normal and my hips have moderate bone loss. There is really no treatment for my condition. The only way to restore bone loss is low impact exercises, or in other words, walking. I need to eat more calcium rich foods and walk briskly for at least 30 minutes four days a week. If I do that my bones should not get worse. So, I can safely say that my future is in my own hands, and I need to be smart about it.

I think I am recovering a little bit because when I feel sad and lonesome, the physical pain is gone. I still miss you every minute of every day, and I continue to look at your empty chair and wish I could share with you the latest news. Last week there were two male deer in the yard and when I saw them I called your name to tell you they were there. It is the first time that bucks have visited us in over a year.

Tomorrow I attend the Hawthorne men's group session. It is rather pleasant and I have met some very nice men. We all have recently lost our wives and we share a common bond. I enjoy the discussions and the social exchange we have.

Thursday is my Grief Recovery meeting. We will discuss the graph I told you about in which we outlined every loss we have had in our life. We will then say a few words about how each loss affected us. What did we feel? How long did it last? And things like that. When I was finished preparing the graph I realized that in my life I did not have too many major losses, and that for 30 years of my life, nothing bad happened. I was excited to learn just how good our life together really was. That fact gave me hope but it also made me very sad and alone. I suppose that confronting my emotions will help me in the long run, but sometimes it is difficult to see where I am going.

I love you more every day and miss you very much.

With all my love,

Lyle

****

Dear Gerda,

Sunday, August 13, 2017: Melinda came up yesterday and spent the night with me and today we went to Howard and Clarissa's celebration. They celebrated 75 years of marriage, Howard's 95th birthday and Clarissa's 90th birthday. There was a crowd of folks there. I had forgotten how big the Handy clan is. Howard has five brothers and one sister, and all of them had several kids. It was fun, but when I looked at the little handout I lost it and started to cry. The opening words were "growing old together." We were going to do that too, but ours got cut short by cancer. Melinda held my hand and I soon stopped, but I was sad the rest of the time.

Melinda and Sophia went on a 14-day vacation, and she had a lot of pictures to show me. They made the road trip through the Southwest and visited Salt Lake City and the Great Salt Lake, Arches NP, Mesa Verde in CO, then on to the Grand Canyon, where they went to the North Rim. That's where we visited when we were there. They spent three days in Los Angeles, and three days in Portland with Ron and Marisa. Most of their trip was during a heat wave. It was well over 100 degrees almost every day. You left instructions for me to help them financially when Melinda got her first vacation, so I did what you told me and gave her $400.00. It helped them a lot, so thank you very much for your love and caring. Melinda cried when I gave her the money and told her about your instructions.

The pain is less but the loneliness is sometimes overwhelming. I can't seem to adjust to the finality of it all, and that life is never going to get better for me, because you are not here to share all of life's little pleasures. I miss that so much.

With all my love
Lyle

****

Dear Gerda,

Monday, I went to Kiwanis today for the first time in over a year. Many of the members gave me a hug and welcomed me back. Most of them also expressed their condolence on your passing. The program that day was Hospice of the Northwest, and I knew two of the speakers. They were both happy to see that I was out in public again and not isolating myself at home. It felt pretty good, and I had a nice lunch. A little bit expensive, but it was the warm meal for the day and I enjoyed it.

Thursday, August 17, I started Mindfulness Meditation at home. I bought a good book that gives detailed instructions how you should meditate for different problems like anxiety, sadness, lack of appetite or insomnia. I don't have lack of appetite or insomnia, but I hope it works for the anxiety I so often have.

The lady from foot care had been ill but was healthy again and Don called and said he had signed me up. I went over and had my toe nails trimmed and my feet massaged. It really felt good. It is so difficult for me to reach my feet because my pot-belly gets in the way. I am trying to lose weight, but is hard not to eat too much when you are sad or lonely.

It is Sunday again and I went to Bethany Covenant. I met Carol Ann and Don there so we sat together and talked a little. Carol's daughter, Barbara, also attends and I talked to her for quite a while before the service started. I don't care much for the music they play in the service, but the pastors are rather good speakers and have a strong message. I will probably keep attending there for the foreseeable future.

Gerda, it is hard to express how much I miss you. The sadness it getting weaker and I am thankful for that. I think the study group is helping me to understand why I am sad, and how to let it go. I will never be the same as we were, but I will one day laugh again.

With all my love,
Lyle

****

Dear Gerda,

It is Sunday, August 27, 2017 and it has been a busy weekend. Yesterday was the High School reunion at the Yacht club in La Conner, the same place you always enjoyed so much. So many of the folks talked to me about you and how much they enjoyed their brief relationship with you. You were a great listener and made the other person feel like they were the only person in the world that counted at that moment. You had that ability, and that is one of the reasons so many folks loved you.

When I got home, Sophia and Melinda came. We went to the Asian Buffet for dinner and enjoyed the evening together. Sophia is such a mature young lady. She is an absolute pleasure to be around. I love her dearly.

We went to La Conner and played tourist for the day. It was kind of fun for a change. We ate fish-and-chips for lunch in the La Conner Tavern. Really good fish. I think it was wild cod, which makes the best fish-and-chips.

Melinda and Sophia left around 4p.m. and Gerald and Betsy stopped by for a couple of hours. They had been in Bellingham and were on their way home. It was nice. We looked at the plum tree and the Italian plums are about ripe. They are right where you liked them, almost ripe but tart. It will be a few more days before they are ripe enough for a good plum cake. Gerald is anxious to try his hand at making one.

Very little happened last week so I haven't written anything to you. I do love you just as much as if I had written every day, and I miss you very much.

I love you.

Lyle

****

Dear Gerda,

Another week has come and gone. September 1st, the third month of being alone came and went. I missed you that day more than I usually do. On Thursday, I attended the grief recovery meeting and shared my homework with the small group. It is amazing how effective the course has been. Many of us were an emotional mess when we started, and now we can talk about things without crying. So much of my sadness has dissolved and I am grateful for that. I pray every day that I will have peace and contentment. I miss you every minute of every day, and I am told that is normal and that it is a good thing. Nothing will ever diminish my love for you, no matter how long I live.

Being alone is not fun, and I look forward to the time when we will be together in heaven. Don't worry, I am not going to do anything to hurry that day up, but I don't look forward to it with fear and anxiety.

It has been very hot for so long that the trees are turning red and losing their leaves at least a month early. I must water the flowers every day. I go outside at eight in the morning before it gets too hot for me to work. I water the flowers and then go for a walk to keep my bones from getting worse. It has been too hot for me to get the lawn and garden in shape, so I will wait for the rain and the cooler air in the fall.

Right now, as I write this, I miss you so much. I love you and think of you often.

With all my love,
Lyle

****

Dear Gerda,

Another week has passed and I am feeling better every week. We finished the grief recovery course and said goodbye to each other. We in the small group have become quite close during the process of sharing our most personal thoughts and emotions. The class helped me so much I am almost afraid to look forward to next week when I don't have the class to attend. I will let you know how it works out. I wrote a poem for the occasion and everyone wanted a copy to take with them, the hospice class coordinator asked if they could use it. I said yes. I included it in the preface to the book.

Today is Don's 86th birthday and Helen invited me to come over for lunch and then Don and I will watch the Seahawks play the Green Bay Packers. It is the first game of the year and both teams are rated about the same, so it should be fun to watch. I promise that I won't yell at the TV when they do something dumb. Well maybe.

I sometimes feel guilty when I don't feel the terrible sadness that I felt before. It has only been three months and everyone told me it would be at least a year for me to recover. I think the time as your caregiver gave me an opportunity to grieve while you were still alive, because I knew how it would end. At this moment, I am happy that the worst pain is gone and I can face your absence without crying.

The plums are ripe and I picked three gallons of them and now need to figure out what to do with them. There are still a lot of plums on the tree, but they are too high up for me to reach them with my six-foot ladder. I am afraid to climb the higher one, and I don't want to fall just for a plum. They are perfect for a cake so Gerald and Steve are coming up on Tuesday and they will make a cake, and we will take it to

Irmgard to share with her and Mike. It will be fun, but I will miss you very much, and it might even be rather painful for us all. We all love you so much.

Health wise I am doing fine. I walk almost every day. I go up the hill and then down to Hickox Road where I go west to the top of the first hill, then I turn around and walk home. It takes me thirty minutes to make the round trip and when I reach the house I am really huffing and puffing. Every day it gets a little easier and I can go a little faster, so it is working and it should be helping my bones to stay strong.

Gerda, I miss you every day and love you unconditionally.

With all my love
Lyle

****

Dear Gerda,

It is now September 17. 2017 and I have kept busy around the place working in the yard. It has been too hot to work after 10a.m. so I go out early and work for an hour or so. This week it cooled off so I was able to work in the morning and then another hour in the afternoon. I still miss you dearly and have no desire to do any of the old things we always shared. I know that I should do them, so I grab myself by the scruff of the neck and outside I go. I assume that that too will get better.

Things are looking better, but I have so much to do, and no desire to do them. I trimmed the rhododendrons and wanted to shred the branches but I couldn't. Last year when I disassembled the chipper/shredder to remove the blockage, I put it back together wrong. I had to tear it apart and reassemble it. I still haven't shredded the pile of stuff.

My life is getting better and I don't have the constant sadness. The worst part is the loneliness. Visiting is fine, but it doesn't satisfy the need. Alone in the evenings and you are not there to share things with. I make my own dinner and then eat alone. News happens and I want to share it with you and I can't. I don't know how long that will last, but it is probably the one-year period everyone talks about. Over all I am fine.

I still miss you a lot, and I think I always will.

With all my love.

Lyle

****

Dear Gerda,

The days keep flying past. For the first three months, time dragged and every day felt like a week. Then suddenly I noticed that time had resumed its pace and was flying once more. I assume that means that I am recovering from your passing. I still miss you just as much as I ever did, and I feel so alone. I wrote the following last Sunday after I watched the Seahawks lose again.

Alone again

Another weekend came and went,
And I am alone again.
The Seahawks played on Sunday
I shouted at the television.
I told them how to play the game
But there was no one to hear me,
For I was alone again.

When I returned from church
The house was empty and dead
No one to talk to. No one
to share my Sunday Dinner.
There was only emptiness,
And I am alone again!

I posted it on Facebook for my friends to see. Several commented on it. I don't put much on Facebook, but four of us from the recovery group set up a group account so we can say things and the whole world can't see it.

Last week I went to see Dr. Creelman and he took a biopsy of a growth on my right ear. He had burned it off three times but it kept coming back. He sent it in to the lab and I will get the results this week. I bled a lot where he took the sample, and of course I got blood all over my pillow that night. I hope it comes out. I also got my flu shot for the winter when I was there.

I don't think I will ever stop missing you. I miss you as intently today as I did the first week following your passing. If you see the good Lord, put in a good word for me. I pray every evening asking Him to take care of you until I get there. You don't need me to take care of you, but I need you by my side and as my loving companion.

I Love you
Lyle

****

Dear Gerda,

It is the first day of October. It has been four months since you passed. I feel terribly low, but the kids helped me.

Ron came up alone on Friday and stayed until Sunday. Saturday, Melinda, Sophia and Gerald were all here. I roasted vegies in the oven and made schnitzel. They turned out very good. Gerald told me they were better than the ones he makes. Who said that you can't teach an old dog new tricks.

When Ron arrived, he cried because you weren't there to greet him. He told me that he misses you every day, but life goes on and he does what he does. He said he cries quite often when he is alone. I felt so sorry for him.

The guy from Handy's Heating came out and serviced the furnace in preparation for winter. He charged me $214.00 for which I wrote a check. He gave me a receipt and lay the check down on the desk. After he left I went in the office and there was the check. He also left one of his tools in the garage, so I took them both out to the store. They were happy to get the check.

Once a month I attend a group at Hawthorne for anyone who is grieving. There is about 20 people attend. They serve a lunch and then a guest speaker talks about items of interest. Mary dee from Avon Church was there and was glad to see me. Also, from Avon was Rob. He was there to offer his services to anyone who might need them. He and Nancy still attend the church in Sedro-Woolley, and are doing fine. It was nice to chat with him a little bit and catch up on everyone.

Saturday was Melissa's birthday. She is the nurse from the clinic with the little short pony tails that we both liked so much. She and I exchange messages every Monday about how the Seahawks performed on Sunday. She is such a lovely person.

I love you and miss you so much. I send you all my love.

Lyle

****

Dear Gerda,

Time is really starting to fly. I guess that is a sign that my life is returning to normal. Whatever normal is.

On Wednesday I met with the attorney and asked him to help me in removing your name from the property. I had asked the person at the records division of the county what I needed to do and she told me so many things that I was completely confused. She told me that most people worked with an attorney. I need to remove your name now so the property will not get all tied up in the legal system when I pass.

I asked Gary at Kiwanis who he would recommend I see and he gave me the name. I liked him. Everything takes time and the property managers at the court house won't take any action until the property taxes for the year are paid. That should happen this month. After I finish this I will need to remove your name from the mortgage and the bank accounts. This is one of the hardest things for me to do. It seems like I am erasing you from my life, and I am not. I miss you and love you as much today as is humanly possible.

Melinda came up again on Saturday and spent the night. I enjoy her visits very much. We now talk about adult things like we never did before. She is about to open her practice. She has all the permits and has found an office space she can afford. She is working on an advertising plan to get her name out there. I offered her some financial help but she declined the offer. She is not quitting her job with the city; she is only going to take clients on a part time basis. I wish her the best of luck. She has dreamed about this for many years, and has worked so hard to finish her education. We can be very proud of our daughter.

I continue to miss you, and love you.

With all my love,

Lyle

****

Dear Gerda,

Another week has come and gone. On Wednesday The Drain Doctor checked out the septic system and found a leaking part in the pumping section. It has rusted though and needed to be replaced. He didn't have the part and didn't have the time to replace it then, so he will return next Wednesday and finish the job. It will be another $400.00 literally down the drain.

Yesterday, October 14th, I went over and visited Howard and Clarissa. I don't think I told you, but Clarissa has cancer of the liver and will not live too much longer. The doctor has not given them any word on how long she has but it won't be long. I visited a couple of weeks ago and she looked fine. Yesterday she looked like skin and bones. She was so happy to see me. We held hands and I told her how much she meant to us and that I loved her from the bottom of my heard. That cheered her up and she laughed for a while. She told me she wanted to do what Gerda had done. "Stop any treatment and put me under Hospice care and let me go." You continue to influence loved ones and others who knew you.

On Friday I packed your shoes in a box and will give them to Goodwill. I thought I was ready to start cleaning out the closet. I was not! When I finished with the shoes I was in tears and knew it was too soon. I did pack up your sleep wear that Helen had bought for you. Helen said she would love to have them, so I will take them to her this week.

I was going to go to church with Don and Helen today, but I got up late and before I could get myself together it was too late. I called and told them to go without me. I will probably go to Bethany Covenant at 11. I haven't gone for the past two weeks because the kids were here.

Preparing for winter, I looked at my sweatshirts and sweaters that were on the shelf in the closet. They were all full of dust. I put them in the dryer and fluffed them. While that was happening, I used the Swiffer duster and cleaned all the shelves. It needed to be done. I looked at your old notes and it is time to wash the curtains. We ignored them for quite a while and throughout the house they are getting dusty and need to be washed. I will probably wait until Melinda comes to help me, and do it then.

I take care of all these things but it seems that life is nothing more than staying alive. I know there is more to life than just not dying, but I haven't found what it is that will give me a purpose.

I love you and miss you very much.

With all my love

Lyle

****

Dear Gerda,

October 15, 2017. After four months and two weeks, life without you has settled into a routine. Sure, I miss you every day, but I have accepted the fact that our life together is finished. I can mourn and worry myself, but nothing I do will bring you back or restore the life we had together. With that acceptance has come a level of peace I haven't had before. I go through the day without sadness and pain and do all the things necessary to sustain myself, and stay healthy. Then something happens and I am confronted with your memory and I plunge into sadness and despair. It only holds my attention for a short time and then it is gone and replaced with the peace and knowledge I had before.

I think some of the peace comes from my practicing of Mindfulness Meditation. It has taught me to focus on the here and now and to forget about the past. The past is gone and there is nothing on earth that can change what has happened. Let it go. The future is also nebulous and no one on earth can tell me what will happen next. I can only prepare myself for what I believe the future holds and live in the moment. What is going to happen will happen, and in most cases, I can't control or change it. Let it happen.

There is a lot more to it than that, but I have learned some great lessons. When I go for my walks, I used to think about everything under the sun, even some very negative thoughts. Meditation has taught me to be mindful of what I am doing. How my feet feel, how the surface of the sidewalk stimulates my feet. How the cool air affects my breath, etc... I have so many things to think about that I don't think about my loss and my emptiness. I am grateful for that and hope that things continue to improve.

I am feeling better, but I miss you every day and always will. I love you and I know I will always love you.

With all my love

Lyle

****

Dear Gerda,

It is Sunday October 22 and I went to church with Don and Helen and then stayed for dinner. Don and I watched the Seahawks play. They won and it was a fun game to watch. I didn't shout at the TV once the entire game. It was a nice day.

Last week Kurt repaired the septic system and replaced the bad part. I was right, the whole event cost me over $415. Nothing is cheap anymore. Also last week I saw Dr. Crowell and she told me my cataracts are ready to be removed. I made an appointment with the surgeon and thought I was ready to have it done, but when I got home I had second thoughts. I am just not ready to do something and I called and cancelled the appointment. I will try it again in January.

I am feeling better but I still have periods of anxiety. I wake up in the morning and start thinking about something and suddenly get anxious. Why I don't know, but my mind can turn anything into a negative experience. It is the old story of borrowing the jack.

Life without you is no fun. I am getting better but I miss you and have so much to tell you and you are not there. I tell you anyway hoping you can hear me.

I send you my love

Lyle

****

Dear Gerda,

Wednesday, November 1st. It has been five months since you passed and today is terrible. I think of you all the time and I miss you so much. I thought I was over the worst of it, but on this day, I am sad and feel like crying. I stopped in at Hospice of the Northwest and gave them some more money that came in from the sale of your book, and when I told the girl about the book I started to cry right there in the office. They didn't seem to notice, so I guess I am not the first person to cry in their office.

Melinda and Ron's birthdays came and went. Ron went to San Francisco for three days over the weekend and visited his friends there. Gerald and Betsy had Melinda over for a nice birthday dinner. The two of them get together a lot and I am pleased that they do. All three of the kids seem to like each other and they seem to be closer than ever before.

At the six month point I will close off the letters and put everything into book form. Hospice wanted me to do that and make it available for anyone who might be in the same circumstances we found ourselves in two years ago. I will keep writing letters to you, but they will be just between us, and will not be made public.

Clarissa is still hanging on to life. I visited her two days ago on Monday, and she was no longer alert and she didn't give any sign that she knew me. I talked to her and told her goodbye and that I loved her as if she were my sister. I think that was the last time I will see her alive. I worry about Howard. Her passing will be terrible for him, and I know it will leave him just a little empty shell with no reason to keep on living. I was only 80 so I could get past it, but at 95 I doubt he will be able to.

I love you and miss you.

Lyle

****

Dear Gerda,

November 10, 2017. All kinds of news and all of it is sad. Clarissa passed away on Friday, November 3rd. She didn't suffer and passed quietly in her bed. Hospice had provided a bed for her and it was set up in the living room so she could be with the family. I will attend her funeral tomorrow, November 11th.

Don S_. also passed away last week, and today is his funeral. He had fallen and his wife found him on the floor. They admitted him to the hospital, and he went back and forth between the hospital and Mira Vista Care Center. He was in the hospital when he died. All of us in club 54 are saddened by his passing. All of us have memories of long conversations with Don. I will miss those calls.

On Wednesday, I went to see Diane Fox and after a full examination, she fitted me with hearing aids. They work, but it will take me a while to get accustomed to them. I will wear these for a week and then she will give me another set and I will have them for a week and compare the two. Then I get to make the decision based on effectiveness and cost. I don't want to pay a ton of money for hearing aids. I may still go to Costco and see what they offer.

It is Monday, November 13th. Friday, I attended Don's funeral at the Salem Lutheran Church in Mount Vernon. It was a very formal church service and most of us felt we had just been to church and heard a good sermon. Tom was there and we agreed that it was too formal, but Alice made the choices and if it was her desire to have it that way, then I will not complain. In any event we were able to pay our respects to him. I think that all of Club 54 were there, and most of them brought their wives.

Sunday was Clarissa's funeral. Melinda and Sophia were still here, so Melinda went with me. It was a beautiful event with reminiscing on the part of the pastor and family. The pastor grew up in Sedro-Woolley and was a friend of Bill's, so he knew Howard and Clarissa very well. The reception was very nice. They put all of Clarissa's collection of salt and pepper shakers on the tables and told everyone to take what they wanted, up to three. Melinda took some and I took an outhouse with a catalog. It was a reminder of my youth.

You would have liked her celebration/funeral. I missed you so much during the entire event. Melinda is such a nice person and she helped me adjust to your absence. I still miss you every day, and I suppose that I will always miss you.

I send you all my love,

Lyle

****

Dear Gerda,

November 21st and it is raining. The weather has been typical November in Washington, wet and gray. For me it is depressing and I must keep the lights on in the house just to survive. It is two more days until Thanksgiving and I don't look forward to it. First, I will drive to Shoreline for the day, but because I don't like to drive after dark, I will stay the night with Gerald and Betsy. I don't like the idea of sleeping in a strange bed and being away from home so I get a little anxious thinking about it.

Yesterday Melinda had surgery on her foot. Her bunion was very painful and needed to be repaired. On top of that when they took x-rays of her foot they bound a piece of broken bone lodged in the joint. When she was working as a bartender several years ago she dropped a keg on her foot and she believes that is where the bone splinter came from.

Sunday was Gerald's 55th birthday and everyone gathered here at our house to celebrate. He and I worked in the kitchen and made leg of lamb just the way you used to do it. It was delicious. Gerald wasn't sure if the lamb would be enough for nine people so he also made a roast beef. It was extremely rare and I didn't even try any.

Betsy brought a small cake and she used just enough candles to form 55. It was a chocolate cake almost like a large brownie.

Ron came up on Friday after work arriving here about 10:30 p.m. He stayed for the entire weekend and we had a real nice visit. Saturday afternoon we visited Irmgard and spent two hours with her. The place was full because they were holding the annual Christmas fair that day. That evening we went to Denny's for dinner. It was surprisingly good.

Whenever we have a family get together I can't stop thinking about you, and then when they all leave I am sad and alone. Yesterday was even worse than usual. Gloria called me at about three in the afternoon and told me that Ray was in the hospital on life support and that later that evening they were going to turn it off and let him pass away. I was in Haggen's super market when I got the call. I started crying right there in the store. It seemed like everyone around me is dying. First Don then Clarissa and now Ray. It hit me so hard because Ray was always so upbeat and happy, always ready to pull a joke on someone. He will be missed by everyone who knew him.

My hearing aids are working and I can watch TV with the volume at a normal level. I have an appointment with Diane at three this afternoon when we will start the third trial period with another hearing aid. When the week is over I will make a decision about what I need and what I can afford.

I have missed you more this past few days than I have in a while. When I think I am getting better, it hits me like a ton of bricks and I am sad and down for a day or two. It is better than it was and I am sure it will continue to get easier as time goes on. In ten more days it will be six months, which is not very long to grieve. I attended a short class on "Surviving the Holidays" which I found very helpful. Hospice has so many things they offer. They are a real godsend.

I love you and miss you so much.

Lyle

****

Dear Gerda,

Today is Sunday November 26. Thanksgiving went very well. I drove down to Shoreline in the pouring rain. It didn't rain the entire way, but enough to make the drive very difficult for me. I made it safely without incident. Ron stayed in Portland with his family, so he sent us a text with pictures of the bird.

Hannah bought a 22-pound turkey at a turkey farm near Bellingham, and it was delicious. I think it was the best turkey I have had in years. Betsy made the same salmon dip and the cheese and cranberry dip that you like so well. I could hardly eat any because every bite reminded me of you and I missed you terribly.

I spent the night and slept well. I had taken my pillow with me, so that helped, but after sleeping in a Tempur-pedic bed all these years, a normal flat mattress took some getting used to. I drove home on Friday and there was no traffic at all. I never slowed down below 60 the entire way.

Friday and Saturday have not been good days. I called Gloria yesterday and talked for a while. Both of us had difficulty talking because we kept crying. It was a very sad conversation. Gloria was reminded of the loss of her daughter and the years of grieving so it is going to be a very difficult time for her. Her son Jimmie came up for Thanksgiving a little early so he has been there with her for the entire time. That was a real blessing for her.

On December 1st it will be six months since you passed. I miss you every day. Some days everything is fine and then I will have a couple of bad days where I miss you so much I can cry at the drop of a hat. It is getting better but I continue to struggle with what I should do with the time I have remaining. Everything I think of leaves me cold, and I don't want to do it. If I could ask you it would help me so much, but that's not possible so I keep on doing my best.

I love you so much and miss you.

All my love

Lyle

****

Dear Gerda,

December 1st. It has been exactly six months since you passed. I expected to feel totally lost today, but it hasn't happened yet. I got up this morning feeling surprisingly good and the sadness has not set in. It may still, but I don't want it to because grieving is so exhausting. I had no idea how much energy it takes just to keep going when you are in grief.

I am going to stop writing for the book on January 1st, 2018. That doesn't mean that I will stop writing to you or thinking about you or missing you. I don't think that will ever happen. I don't want to stop missing you, but I want it to be in a positive way. I have so many wonderful memories of you and that will always be with me no matter what I do.

I send you all my love

Lyle

****

Dear Gerda,

December 21, the first day of winter. It is projected to get very cold for the Christmas weekend, but no snow or freezing rain, so the kids will be able to make it here for the weekend. I put up all the Advent decorations around the 10th of December and then decorated the tree the next day. I knew that you would want me to do things as much as we did before and so I just did it. It was painful to think that this would be the way it is going to be, but I got it done.

Gerald and his family along with Melinda and Sophia will be here Christmas Eve, and Melinda and Sophia will stay overnight. Earlier this week I made sugar cookies and a bunch of the spicy walnuts. They turned out really good. I have herring for Gerald and Melinda, and we will heat a ring of fleischwurst for the rest of us. I am picking up potato salad from Haggen's and I have all the ingredients to make the noodle salad you made. I think you got it from Helen. I want to do everything the same way you did, including a tray of snacks to eat during the rest of the evening.

We will all miss you like crazy, but it will be a time of love and caring for you and for each other. Together we raised some wonderful children who have become the nicest adults anyone could wish for. They all dearly love you and I love them in return.

I will finish the book for Hospice on the 1st of January, but I will continue to write to you because I want to. Somehow it gives me peace to share with you the things that have happened since you passed on to Heaven. It gives me peace to know that you are in a safe place and waiting for me to arrive.

I love you and miss you so much

All my love

Lyle

****

Dear Gerda,

January 1, 2018. Christmas went exactly as planned. We ate dinner and then shared our gifts. I got my puzzle to work and Sophia got a lot of nice things. I gave her $200 which she will put to good use. Gerald and I arranged the platter, I sliced some French bread and we all dug in. The way we attacked the platter you would think we had not eaten anything. The night was perfect except that you were not there. Ron called with "Facetime" so we could all see each other and all the decorations. He made the tour of the house and showed us the tree, the gifts, and we did the same.

New Years was nice. Ron and family came up on Saturday and went home on Monday the first. Melinda came up on the 31st and we spent the evening watching TV. Melinda's friend in Germany who had been fighting cancer died on Friday and she was bummed out and sad all evening. For her it was a sad night, missing you and grieving for her very close friend. I felt so bad that there was nothing I could do to help her. You never get over being a parent.

I made herring for Ron and for dinner I made schnitzel with mixed peppers and fried O'Brian potatoes. I am getting pretty good in the kitchen. I had planned to make the American brunch like you always did for Monday, but Ron asked me not to. The knowledge that you were not there made him sad and he knew that if I made breakfast he would sit there and cry. I changed the menu and we had cold cuts and bread. We had plenty to eat and it helped Ron get through the day.

Today it has been seven months. Somehow my grief has subsided and I am not anxious any longer. Just before Christmas the pastor's sermon was on Philippians 4:6-9. It was exactly what I needed to hear and it has helped me a great deal the last few weeks.

> *"6 Be anxious for nothing, but in everything by prayer and supplication with thanksgiving let your requests be made known to God. 7 And the peace of God, which surpasses all comprehension, will guard your hearts and your minds in Christ Jesus.*
>
> *8 Finally, brethren, whatever is true, whatever is honorable, whatever is right, whatever is pure, whatever is lovely, whatever is of good repute, if there is any excellence and if anything worthy of praise, dwell on these things. 9 The things you have learned and received and heard and seen in me, practice these things, and the God of peace will be with you."*

I will continue to miss you and love you until then.

As far as the book is concerned it is Auf Wiedersehen. Until I see you in Heaven and we are once again joined in love and happiness.

I love you
Lyle

ENDING

My period of grieving is coming to an end, at least as far as this book is concerned. I will continue to grieve in private, and I will keep on writing my journal, but it will remain private. The sadness has retreated to a place where it doesn't bother me like it did. I am happy that my thinking has returned to normal and I can face each new day with a sense of hope.

I am now faced with the task of downsizing the house and disposing of many of the things that were hers. What do I do with her clothes, her jewelry, and the thousand other things that remind me of her? Can someone use them? Should I take everything to Goodwill? What should I do? There is no rule that states I must take care of these things now. There is no right or wrong way to do it, and no one can tell me when or how. Only I can decide what is right for me and my family. No matter what I decide, the act of sorting and letting go will be painful.

I will continue trying to find my purpose for being here. Trying to find the activity that fulfills my needs and my desires. Will I find it? I don't know, but I must continue the search.

I spent two years focusing on one thing: caring for my wife. Every thought, every task, everything I did 24 hours a day, seven days a week, all were focused on her welfare and

Lyle E. Herbaugh

comfort, both physical and mental. Every fiber of my being was tuned into the task at hand, and I knew why I was here. I knew what I was supposed to do and I did it. When you have been dedicated to one thing for so long, it is almost impossible to disconnect and direct your thinking to something else which by comparison, seems so unimportant.

When I think of all the things that were, good and bad, and all of things that can never be again, I know that I must let them go to their rightful place in my memory. All that remains is now and I must live today, enjoy whatever time I have left and let everything else go. That may be the most difficult task of all!

Lyle E. Herbaugh

ABOUT THE AUTHOR

Lyle grew up on a farm in rural Washington where he learned about hard work, and developed a work ethic that helped him succeed throughout his working years. When he was nineteen he enlisted in the Air Force and served for fourteen years. In 1959 he was assigned to Wiesbaden, Germany where he met his wife Gerda. They were married in 1960. Lyle continued to work for the Air Force for over 40 years, with four assignments in Germany totaling 28 years. He retired in 1995 and now lives in Mount Vernon, Washington. Gerda passed away June 1st 2017.